ELIZABETH

M000020496

Walking
in my
SHOES

Blessing on
your journey
Elizabeth Mitchell

I had a dream.
But what God had in mind
was so much bigger.

"To look at Elizabeth, you wouldn't guess she's covered as much ground as she has—her calm beauty doesn't reveal the tragedy and heartache, the incredible pain, or anything else she's left behind to pursue her Savior. But in this remarkable book, we discover the real story that has shaped the woman we all know and love today.

My friend Elizabeth beckons us to join her on a remarkable journey that gives us a truly personal look at a woman whose character has been tested and honed by grit and grace. I heartily recommend it!"

—Joni Eareckson Tada
Joni and Friends International Disability Center

"'Everybody has a story,' says the author in this wonderful book. But I would add: few have such a story of courage, faith, and heart love for Jesus lived out in pain with such shouts of victory.

I witnessed a stadium full of Eastern European women in Budapest, Hungary. Women stood to their feet to greet her as she came to the platform to speak; most were in tears. They were making a standing statement of the spiritual lifeline that the editor of Lydia magazine had been to them through the years.

As we are reminded here, 'Experience from the past gives us courage for the present task!' Thank you, Elizabeth."

—Jill Briscoe
Author and Speaker

"Elizabeth has a compelling personal story, and for years I have urged her to tell it. Now she has written *Walking in My Shoes*, and it's a powerful and vulnerable account of her life journey. It will bring tears, hope, and joy to all who read it. When I think of Elizabeth, my mind goes to a beautiful church stained glass window (see chapter 24), and I say of her: 'She is colorful, transparent and the Son shines through her!'"

—Dr. George O. Wood
President of the World Assemblies of God

"I am intimately familiar with Elizabeth's extraordinary journey from a childhood on a humble farm in former communist Yugoslavia to the fulfillment of a lifelong dream to impact her world through the printed page. In this fast-paced and inspiring book, you will travel with her as she grows from a simple girl with a treasured pencil to the founder and editor of a major Christian magazine touching the lives of hundreds of thousands of readers throughout the world. Filled with spiritual insights learned along the way, this book will encourage those whose dreams are faltering and give strength to those already traveling the road of faith."

—Sharon Mumper
President, Magazine Training International

"Grab your comfortable shoes and walk a very uncomfortable path with Elizabeth Mittelstaedt through a life of challenges. At each stop, you'll change to another pair of shoes so you can truly "walk a mile in her shoes" through Communist and post-Communist Europe. This autobiographical journey keenly takes the reader through each step and creatively lets the metaphor of shoes do the walking for the reader. Elizabeth's rough road always had the divine Sojourner, Jesus, as her traveling companion, often carrying her along the path and through treacherous obstacles. Though a different time and culture, her superbly written "walk" offers readers a depth of understanding for the road called life."

—Dr. Marla Campbell
Professor Emeritus, Biola University
Teacher/Trainer, Assemblies of God World Missions

"So much history in one person's life. Through epic world events and continents, Elizabeth's odyssey reads like a novel—but is the true story of a single individual's life. It's the story of a woman who, with determination, pursues her path with God and humanity. For decades, she has given women hope, comfort, and courage throughout the world through her ministry as editor and publisher. Here is a life that is must-reading."

—Dr. Christoph Fasel
Former Chief Editor of
Reader's Digest *Germany and Austria*

"Elizabeth is a powerful light and source of inspiration across all of Western and Eastern Europe. She has truly lived with passion and purpose, even when doing so has been far from easy. *Walking in My Shoes* chronicles her journey through multiple painful obstacles with great vulnerability, sensitivity, steely strength, and an unstoppable determination to risk everything to follow God and the passionate purpose He has instilled in her soul. All who read this story of remarkable courage, hope, and resilience will marvel—and find healing and encouragement for their own journeys."

—Dr. Joan Funk, PhD

"I was captivated from the first page. I felt as if I was swept along in wide-eyed wonder for the entire journey through this true tale. Elizabeth's life is evidence that God's love for His children is tender and relentless."

Robin Jones Gunn
Best-selling author of the
Christy Miller *series and* Victim of Grace

"There are living examples that confirm the claim that physical suffering produces spiritual gems. Elizabeth's hard life journey and her phenomenal success convincingly testify to the transformational power of faith, love, and perseverance.

Fragile and humble, but always charmingly dignified and creatively entrepreneurial, with a bright mind and a noble character, Elizabeth was a consistent witness for the cross, which speaks of love more than suffering. She became the editor of one of the most widely read women's magazines in Europe. That confirms the words of Mother Theresa that pain and suffering make sense only if they bring us so much closer to Jesus that we can hear His whisper and understand His plan for our life.

Elizabeth not only heard it but also realized it, and we, her friends, wish to thank her that in her international success, she has not forgotten her native region of former Yugoslavia."

—Dr. Peter Kuzmic
Distinguished Professor of
World Missions and European Studies,
Gordon Conwell Theological Seminary

Walking in My Shoes
Trilogy Christian Publishers A Wholly Owned Subsidary of Trinity Broadcasting Network
2442 Michelle Drive Tustin, CA 92780

10 9 8 7 6 5 4 3 2 1

Library of Congress Cataloging-in-Publication Data is available.

ISBN: 978-1-64773-949-2
E-ISBN: 978-1-64773-950-8

DEDICATION

*To all the women who have helped me
become the woman I am:
The women who were not afraid
to follow God's calling in their lives
and who encouraged me to follow my God-given dream.*

PREFACE

What's Your Story?

After decades of secrecy,
I finally learned the truth about who I was.

————————

Each of us has a story to tell—a story of life-changing events, small and large, that should pass from generation to generation and to all who will listen. Some of our life stories may be dramatic, like jagged mountains and valleys on a bar graph. Others may seem like linear lines with little movement, little change. But only our loving God knows the end of our stories and how they will influence others along the way. The question is, *will you risk telling your story?* Will you share your heart and your life experiences so that others may see what it's like to have walked a mile in your shoes? So that through your experience, they may gain courage and strength for walking a mile in their own shoes?

Walking in My Shoes is my life's legacy. A story of humble beginnings, traumatic events, world-shaking change, decades of secrecy, pain and joy, betrayal and love, passion and purpose. A tale of times when God saved my life, and I wondered, *Why? For what reason? What does God have in mind for me? Does my life matter?*

Dear friend, do you wonder the same things? If your life matters? If you matter? Are you asking questions about your role in your family, your neighborhood, your country, the world? Do you find yourself doubting that you could do anything meaningful, even if you tried? Do you live in fear because of your daily circumstances? Do your limitations dishearten you? By events in your past that hold you back?

Walking in My Shoes is my life story. But it's also much more. I pray you will find hope for your life questions and inspiration to begin, or continue, pursuing your dreams. For how do you know what you can accomplish unless you try?

I know what can happen, through the grace of God, for I've been there. And I'm still, day by day, walking in these shoes. Life is sometimes tricky, and I can get bogged down in the mud. Other times, I am "surprised by joy," as the esteemed author C.S. Lewis was, and I find my feet barely reaching the earth.

Walking in My Shoes is a story of the times when God opened doors that seemed impossible to open. Of times when I was wounded, in unfathomable pain, and could only cry out to God for His grace and mercy. It is a story of those moments when the Lord met me in my greatest need and showed the pathway to fulfilling my greatest dreams and more.

He can do the same for you. His grace and healing await.

—Elizabeth Mittelstaedt

ACKNOWLEDGMENTS

While meeting with a few ladies for coffee in 1985 in Santa Ana, California, I shared one of my cow stories (now included in this book). One of these dear friends smiled and handed me an empty journal. "Elizabeth," she said, "you have to write." To my great surprise, a year later, *Lydia* magazine was born, and I did begin to write—the editorial! The rest of the pages, I left to women from all walks of life to tell their transformational stories.

In the last years, God impressed upon my heart to begin making notes about my own life story, thinking that someday God would lead me to share with others in book form, maybe?

I could never have completed this project without my dear friend, Ramona Tucker. Our paths crossed by divine intervention when she was Editor of *Today's Christian Woman* magazine, and she invited me to be the back page columnist.

A special thanks to Robin Jones Gunn and Paula Gamble: how I appreciate your countless questions and excellent, creative suggestions.

To my husband Ditmar: our journey together of over forty-nine years—including Vancouver, Los Angeles, Chicago, Frankfurt, Berg-hausen, and back to California—has indeed been an adventure. This book would never have happened without your help.

TABLE OF CONTENTS

PROLOGUE

Escape to Freedom

"Once we cross this mountain, you will be free!"

FALL 1963

The cool evening mist moistened my cheeks as Tamas, my guide to freedom, approached the densely wooded slopes of the Austrian Alps. We didn't have mountains like this in northeastern Yugoslavia, and I felt dwarfed in their shadow. They loomed before us like giants guarding an ancient castle.

"That is where we need to go," Tamas said and pointed to a mountaintop where there were no more trees. "Once we cross this mountain, you will be free!"

I couldn't believe we were so close. My heart slammed against my chest, half from fear, half from excitement. With hurried breaths and quickened steps, we ducked into the forest, hoping the police had not seen us.

The higher in altitude we climbed, the colder it became. I wore only a light jacket, and it felt as if the wind was pelting my bare skin. My teeth started to chatter. While my feet fought their way through the thicket of the forest to stay on the narrow path, my lungs filled with the cold, thinning air—and the musty scent of moss, mushrooms, and fallen leaves. Once so wonderfully alive and colorful, the foliage now smelled of death.

For a brief moment, I wondered if that would be the outcome of this journey—my death attempting to flee communism. The grueling nature of the walk soon drove away thoughts from my mind except putting one foot in front of the other to stay on the path.

After a while, the mist thickened into what felt like raindrops. I was sure I would shrivel and disintegrate like the autumn leaves I was tramping on. Every inch of me was soaked through, doubling the weight of my frail, seventeen-year-old frame. Drops ran down my waist-long, light brown hair like a little stream. The ever-increasing mud was caking my shoes as we trudged ever so slowly through the mountain forest. My feet ached until numbness set in. Still, we kept marching on.

Finally, I was sure my feet would take me no farther. "Please, let's stop!" I pleaded with Tamas.

"No," he said, shaking his head. "We must continue."

And he marched resolutely on. I paused for an instant, then summoning up all my strength, I forged ahead, following him blindly.

The sun disappeared almost completely, and darkness invaded the forest. Soon we could see only the trees as silhouettes in the moonlight. Without a clear vision, my ears took over. Every little crack in the woods seemed to indicate impending danger. Birds' shrill evening cries made my stomach cringe. Back home, I had relished the darkness as a rest from work. But tonight, there would be no rest. There was only uncertainty and fear.

It was the longest, loneliest night I'd ever experienced. I couldn't help but wonder if I had made the right choice. Yet now, I was committed to it. There was no going back, no changing my mind.

By dawn, we had almost reached the mountain peak. We were still in the forest, but just beyond us, there were no more trees. On our far left, I spotted a watchtower. A uniformed guard carrying a rifle was walking toward it.

"See that guard?" Tamas pointed ahead. "That's the border into Austria. From here on, we need to crawl so he won't see us. We'll go to the border first and then across the last meters of no-man's-land."

Ah, that must be the five hundred meters belonging to neither country, Yugoslavia or Austria, I remembered. I looked at Tamas—tall, skinny, dark-haired, in his twenties. When our eyes met, I saw a slight hesitancy there, but somehow he remained calm.

How does he know all these details? I wondered. *Has he done this before?* He acted like he knew exactly how to go about crossing the border. He told me that we would have to crawl for almost four hundred meters from the edge of the woods to reach Austrian ground—and our freedom. My heart was beating faster than I thought was possible.

"Ready?" he whispered.

I bit my bottom lip and nodded.

Then, suddenly, several guards emerged from the watchtower and began to walk toward us.

Had we been spotted? Were we about to be captured and interrogated?

A rush of blood throughout my body fueled my panic. Tamas panicked, too. I noticed a thin line of sweat on his brow. He turned to me abruptly and whispered, his dark eyes intense, "You believe in God! Would you please talk to Him? Ask Him to help us so the soldiers won't see us!"

"Please, God," I prayed quietly and frantically aloud, "help us cross the border safely. And please, make sure the soldiers don't see us."

When we looked up, the guards were walking back toward the tower. *A coincidence,* I wondered, *or God's miracle?*

Tamas seized the moment. "Now," he said, motioning with his head toward the border. Flattening himself, he began to crawl toward the crossing.

I was already soaking wet. The feel of sloppy mud on my hands and knees was less of a concern than my troubled thoughts: *Were land mines hidden in the ground? Would it hurt to be shot? Would these be the last moments of my life?*

Once again, I asked myself, *Why am I so hungry for freedom? Why am I risking my life to cross the border? Why am I leaving my family and all I know behind in this search for something more?*

But the hunger for freedom had been fierce within me for a long time, desiring to be released. It was something I could not ignore. I knew I could no longer stay under the thumb of communism. I wasn't sure precisely what freedom meant. I needed to be free to make choices from my soul. I longed for that "something more" in my life, and I was determined to do all I could to help bring it about.

That passion for purpose and meaning had grown in my heart until it was so solidly entrenched, deep within me, that I had decided to escape Yugoslavia. I would make my way to freedom. And Tamas had seemed like my ticket out.

But now, the reality of what the journey meant hit home. I found myself in the range of gunfire, crawling through the mud toward an uncertain border crossing. And I was petrified.

Concentrating on the ground before me, I didn't dare to look up. The sight of Tamas's muddy feet in front of me was my only lifeline. *Was I breathing or holding my breath?* I wasn't sure. My body was moving, but everything else critical to life seemed suspended.

You can't see political boundaries in dirt or grass, but at some point, we left communist Yugoslavia and entered free Austria.

Now, standing far beyond the watchtower and the range of gunfire, the sky seemed bluer, the air fresher.

"We made it!" I whispered while gazing at the vast, windswept meadows on what seemed like the top of the world. For the first time in hours, my breathing returned to a semi-normal cadence.

Suddenly, we came upon a little cabin with a sign, "Welcome to Austria"!

I smiled and wondered, *Who would have thought to put a little hut up here to welcome foreigners like me? How many had done this before me?* I looked over to the mountains and marveled: This is where freedom lives.

With the help of my guide, I had just accomplished something that thousands of my countrymen only dreamed of: I had left my old life under communism and oppression behind and crossed into the West, the land of freedom and opportunity.

I breathed deeply of the fresh mountain air. Here I would pursue my dreams of education and all that my heart told me to be. I would live fiercely and fully.

ELIZABETH MITTELSTAEDT

Little did I know, at that euphoric moment, that my freedom would turn out to be short-lived. Or that soon I would enter into a nightmare I would battle for years to come…one so much worse than everything I'd already endured.

PRINCESS SHOES AND PENCILS

*There were two possessions I cherished as a child:
a pair of shoes, and a pencil.*

"Our family hasn't always been poor," my mother told me when speaking of our life before communism. As she talked about "the good old days," her face lit up with a bright smile, and her eyes shone with joy. "We used to have servants and a fine horse-drawn carriage," she said. "And I wore beautiful cashmere sweaters and satin dresses." My mother's posture straightened as if she were, indeed, wearing an elegant gown instead of a simple house dress.

"Why don't we have these things now?" I asked.

My mother's face grew sad as she explained, "Under communism, everyone is supposed to be equal."

We lived in a small Hungarian village called Ludas in the province of Vojvodina. This province was autonomous within Serbia. It was tucked away in the northeast corner, bordering on Hungary and Romania. Throughout history, the fiery storms of continual change were tearing this province, and the people lived under varied political, cultural, economic, and social conditions. After World War II ended in 1945, Josip Broz Tito became the leader of Yugoslavia. When his communist party took over the government, my family—like so many others—lost most of its possessions.

Despite the poverty, I found riches in my environment and nature. I loved our village, which curved around a beautiful lake where birds, frogs, and fish felt as at home as Grandpa did in our town in which he'd lived for more than half a century.

Our family of eleven lived in a simple yellow house. Since we had no indoor plumbing, we used a wooden outhouse in our backyard.

Under the roof of our long, yellow house, *Nagyapa* (Grandpa) and *Nagyanya* (Grandma) lived on one side, and my mother, father, and we, seven girls, lived on the other side. I had two older sisters and four younger ones. On a summer evening, my sisters and I would listen as the frogs gave a concert. They would "sing" so loudly that overnight guests (somehow we always managed to squeeze them in) kept complaining: "We can't sleep!" My sisters and I, however, were not kept awake by the frog-songs. We loved them; they were our nighttime lullaby.

During my childhood summers, I loved to run and play barefoot along the dusty roads (I didn't realize until later that Mother welcomed our bare feet because then we weren't wearing out our shoes) when I wasn't doing chores. Each sister had her duties to do. Mine, as a child in the middle of the herd, was to tend the geese and cows.

When the sun reached a certain point each evening, I knew it was time to herd the cows home to be milked.

I could hardly wait to finish, so we children were at last free to play. I would get together with the neighbor kids to play hide-and-seek. We would play until it was very dark, then Mother would call us in for supper. Then, as soon as we finished washing the dishes, we'd be off to sleep.

Snuggled warmly in my bed, surrounded by my siblings, I would gaze out the window at the millions of stars, so bright and beautiful, and feel that I was living in a veritable wonderland. There was a universe much bigger than I knew...one that I eagerly wished to explore.

Some of my happiest childhood times were listening to stories. These stories gave me a vision of a bigger world and an identity beyond our small village. I found treasures in the stories I heard and used them to feed my mind and soul.

On a winter evening, in the dim light of a kerosene lamp, our family would sit around that warm clay stove, listening to Grandma's fairy tales. When she began with "once upon a time," I snuggled in closer and listened intently. She introduced me to the worlds of Cinderella, Snow White, and Sleeping Beauty. My absolute favorite story was Snow White. I didn't need a picture book, which was a good thing since we didn't have one. I used my imagination to picture what she must have looked like. In my mind's eye, Snow White was a most beautiful princess.

But some parts of the story made me sad. *Why did her mother have to die? And why was her stepmother not nice to her?* "Why didn't somebody protect her?" I asked Grandma.

Grandma sighed. "That's just how the story goes," she said. "Sometimes, real life is like that too. Bad things do happen to good people. But it doesn't mean that the ending has to be sad."

I pondered over her words that night, never dreaming that, someday, I would deeply understand their true meaning.

There were two possessions I cherished as a child: a pair of shoes and a pencil. These small treasures seemed enough for my carefree, childish heart—at least for a while. But now I recognize those little items for the symbols they would become in my life.

When I was seven, I received my first pair of brand-new shoes: simple, black, slip-on shoes. Before that, I'd always worn hand-me-downs, so it was no surprise that I cared for them as if they were my most precious possession. When I wore them, I felt like a princess from one of my grandmother's stories. I would carry them to school and then, right before turning into the schoolyard, would slip them on, making sure nobody was looking. After school, I wore them just out of sight of the schoolyard, then took them off again and carried them home. I didn't want them to wear out!

What I hadn't realized was how soon those princess shoes would be too small for my growing feet. Since we didn't have money to purchase new ones, my mother cut a hole in the end of my shoes to make room for my long toes.

My second childhood treasure was my pencil. It needed to last me for a long time. This bashed-up pencil was so precious to me because

I loved to write. From the young age of eight, when we memorized a poem by Sándor Petőfi, I had been dreaming of becoming a writer. This gifted, nineteenth-century Hungarian poet had used the printed page to fight for freedom of speech, the press, and religion. His passion captivated me. Even as a child, I was deeply impressed with the power of the printed page.

Since I was limited to one pencil, and my creative impulse yearned to be released, I had to find other ways to write my words. In the summer, I scribbled in the dust—poems, stories, and whatever else came to my mind. The big advantage? There was always plenty of dust around, and my feet worked just fine as an eraser. In the winter, the snow became my "page." The frost quickly turned my fingers into little icicles, but even the cold could not stop me from writing. I dreamed of becoming a writer who would influence others and change my world.

The treasured pencil was a foreshadowing of my lifelong dream, symbolizing the passion God had instilled in me at such an early age.

A JUMBLE OF SHOELACES

*I was torn between what I really believed
and what I had to say to please my communist teachers.*

How powerful the written word is! More than sixty years after the death of Karl Marx, we were studying his writings in a small village school in Ludas. Like the rest of the students, I listened intently as my teachers spoke enthusiastically about his communist ideology of a new and better world.

"There are only two dangers to human happiness," Karl Marx wrote: "different social classes and religion." His father, Levi Marx, who had grown up in a Jewish rabbi's family in Prussia, converted to Christianity so he would be allowed to practice law. His son, Karl, departed even further from the family tradition. He became an atheist and spent his whole life arguing against religion and capitalism. "Religion is a daydream," he wrote. "A tranquilizer that causes humankind to passively endure the pain of today in the hope of heaven tomorrow. After capitalism has enslaved the people, they need religion to give them hope."

Karl Marx's calling was to rally the simple workers and poor people (the "Proletarians") to fight and rid themselves of the capitalist chains. His slogan was: "Proletarians of the world, unite!" In the storm of a communist revolution, he said the rich and powerful (whom he called "Bourgeoisie"—a nightmare for all dyslexic people) tremble. And tremble they did. In many countries of the world, such as my homeland of Yugoslavia, the communists took over the government. They robbed the wealthy of all their possessions and created a "planned economy," a society where all were supposedly "equal" in status. Finally, I understood why my family had lost some of our land, horses, carriage, and fancy clothes.

But I found communism very confusing. Karl Marx had promised freedom, yet thousands upon thousands of people died. He promised a better world without religion and social classes. Yet, there was a vast disparity between the ordinary people (like my family now) and the communist party leadership. People were to trust and obey the "party" without question. (Evidently, the communists wanted to save the people the trouble of thinking!) "For the greater good of the community, the individual must step back," they taught. "In the party, each one of us must sacrifice our rights."

General Tito, the president of Yugoslavia, had something in common with Karl Marx. Both had grown up in religious homes. Tito served in the church as an altar boy. But Tito's view of religion was influenced by an experience he'd had in the church as a young boy. One day, during his church duties, he accidentally spilled the communion wine. The officiating priest slapped him and shouted, "Leave! Don't come back!" Tito never returned.

With all its different ethnic peoples, six socialist republics, and two autonomous provinces, under President Tito's rule, Yugoslavia became one unified country under the Federal People's Republic of Yugoslavia in 1946. After Tito's death in May 1980, unrest spread across the country. Starting in 1991, the Balkan Wars broke out. Since then, the republics have become independent countries Slovenia, Croatia, Macedonia, Bosnia-Herzegovina, Montenegro, and Serbia.

In spite of my meager existence growing up, I was somehow blessed with a natural optimism. I adapted quickly to situations and enjoyed life to the full.

But I increasingly felt torn between what I believed to be true in my heart and what I was allowed to say publically.

School should have been a safe place to explore the truth. But I soon discovered that we were not free to voice our opinions or ask questions, let alone object or disagree. It was not allowed. Living under communism was all about "group think"—not what you, as an individual, thought. So I learned to keep quiet.

I knew I was not free to state my doubts and questions, which were many:

- *Why is it wrong to believe in God?*
- *How do you know He doesn't exist?*
- *Why aren't we allowed to travel?*
- *Why are the capitalists evil?*
- *Why can't I ask these questions?*

Being so full of questions and not allowed to voice them was disconcerting. In my mind, I was free to say what I wished, to hope, to pray, to dream. But outwardly, I had to say what pleased my teachers. It created inner turmoil that I could never escape.

Even at home, there was conflict because of communism and all the rules, both spoken and unspoken.

My parents advised, "We must stay silent!"

But my grandmother vehemently disagreed. "We need to be bold! A system without God cannot work. The fear of the LORD is the beginning of wisdom."

Who was I to believe? My beloved grandma, my parents, or my teachers? I wanted to please my teachers, yet I had to hide my love for God when I was with them.

At school, I often looked at the world map with deep interest. *What would it be like to visit another country?* I wondered. *What does America look like? Are the people friendly? What would it be like to be "free"? To go where I want, say what I want, think what I want—without the worry of reprisal?*

These inner conflicts led to false guilt. Suppose I did not support the philosophy of communism. Wasn't I betraying my home country and all its people? After all, they labeled people who escaped across the border as enemies and traitors.

Because I grew up in a communist system, I learned to keep some things—my true beliefs and feelings—hidden deep inside. I learned to be cautious. Sometimes that has served me well in my adult life. At other times this extra caution has limited me.

Even today, I continue to become more aware of hidden pieces inside me—ones I don't even know exist until I am surprised by a memory. Then, for me, healing comes in finding words for the undefined secrets of the soul. As I write my sometimes fragile feelings, I gain clarity and understanding.

One of my most cherished memories is the special summers when for a few weeks, my mother allowed me to visit my sister, Edit, nine years older than me. She lived with my Aunt Erzsébet (Elizabeth) in the distant city of Ada, about four hours' ride by train from my hometown. My aunt Elizabeth was also my godmother. She had no children.

I enjoyed those summers at my aunt's house so much! While there, I didn't have my usual home chores of tending the geese and cows. At Aunt Elizabeth's house, my only task was to fetch drinking water from a fountain a few streets away.

But one thing was puzzling. Each time I walked past the neighbor's house, with water pail in hand, I would see a man and a boy at the window watching me intently. Then, one day, Beni, this neighbor boy, came over to play with me.

Summer after summer, Beni continued to come over to play. I enjoyed his company very much.

One summer day, though, I saw Beni in a different light. As he entered the door, I glanced at his handsome face, and my heart skipped a beat. He had grown so tall and muscular.

He is so handsome! I thought. I'd seen him many times before, and we'd nearly grown up together in the summer, but this time I noticed him. His blond hair and blue eyes—so like mine.

Quickly Beni became my childhood sweetheart. Yet when we reached our teens, my aunt began to worry about me, especially after I told her, "I like Beni, and one day I will marry him."

"You can marry anybody else in the whole wide world, but not Beni," she told me sharply.

Why? I wondered. *Why not Beni?*

But I didn't say anything, of course. I knew better than to question my aunt.

It would be years before I learned the secret about Beni.

Our village school ended after grade school. To continue further education, I would have to go to the city about an hour's walk away. I dreamed of becoming a teacher who would inspire children and make a contribution to society. I couldn't wait until the city school started.

My father, though, did not want to pay for a "second household" in the city. In the winter, it would be difficult to walk that far in the snow, he said. Furthermore, he had an old-fashioned opinion about women and education. "Why does a girl need more education?" my father asked bluntly. "You will get married and raise children just like your two older sisters." His sharp tone and solemn face made it clear: no more questions!

When my father said no, that settled it. I'd learned from early on that my father's no was always set in concrete. Still, I was so passionate about my dream that I didn't give up easily. I argued; I cried; I begged; I made all kinds of promises. All was in vain. I could not convince him to see it from my point of view. I turned to my mother for help, but she would not say anything. I was devastated. But what could I do? My dream was about to die before it even had a chance to launch.

When my teachers found out that my parents weren't going to let me continue with my schooling, they came to our house and begged them to reconsider. "She's very bright—our best student," they said, "and a scholarship will be waiting for her."

But my father had made up his mind. *"Nem!"* No.

Sadly, I watched my teachers leave. That night I cried into my pillow and asked, "Why?" over and over.

I also felt disappointed. *It's because I'm a girl*, I thought bitterly. *If I were a boy, this wouldn't have happened. Why did God have to make me a girl?*

My tear-stained pillow brought no relief for my shattered dreams.

A few days later, I took my pencil and a sheet of paper, hoping to fill it with a poem about my broken dreams of becoming a teacher. But nothing came. At the young age of twelve, they stole my passion for teaching from me, and I was staring at a blank, white page.

GIFT TO CHERISH

In fairy tales, the story always had a happy ending.
But what about my life?

"Forget about school!" Mother said, "Go now, and pick *majva*!"

Majva (hollyhock) was an assortment of lilac flowers that grew in the summer. The blossoms were dried and used for medicinal purposes; we sold them once a week.

Mother always planted enough majva bushes to produce tedious work all summer long. My sisters and I loathed these flower bushes that towered over us at over six feet tall. It was essential to pick the flowers daily, for by evening the blossoms would close and fall off. The next day, new blooms would appear, and it was imperative we pick them in the middle of the day when the temperature soared to the mid-80s. If we didn't pick the flowers then, we'd lose them. The job was always urgent but never finished.

Occasionally, Mother would take pity on us. "Go swim in the lake and cool off," she'd say. "But come back quickly!"

Even worse than the sunburns, though, were the bee stings. Far too often, while bees were in the flower collecting nectar, we'd grab the flower and get stung. Hardly a day went by when I didn't get stung on the hand, sometimes even twice. But what kept us going, summer after hot summer, was Mother's promise that if we picked a lot of flowers, she'd buy each of us a lovely dress for school.

This year, though, I knew I wouldn't be going back to school. My father dashed my dreams of becoming a teacher. I couldn't imagine anything but a dismal future; never-ending summers of acres of majva bushes stretched across my mind's eye. In fairy tales, the story always had a happy ending. *But not in my life,* I thought sadly. *My life is as ugly as my sunburnt hand stung by bees.*

One winter evening, my aunt Ilonka visited us, and over dinner, she told us how excited she was about a discovery she had made.

"In the past, I wasn't sure if God existed," my aunt began. "If He did, and there was a heaven, how do you get there? How can you be good enough? Then I met a couple who told me that Jesus had already paid for all my sins on the cross—that He died for us, in our place. To get to heaven, all I needed to do was ask Him to forgive my sins and to receive Jesus as my Savior. The exciting news is that God desires to have a relationship with His children, whom He created, and that anyone who repents of wrongdoing and sin and chooses to trust in God will inherit heaven."

We looked at her in disbelief. *How could this be?*

"What do you mean, receive Jesus?" my father asked, appearing confused.

"Man and God are separated," Aunt Ilonka explained. "The Bible says, 'There is no one righteous, not even one.'[1] We have all sinned, and no matter how many good works we do, we can never be good enough to please God. If we could save ourselves, then why would God let His only Son die on the cross?" It was a new thought for us.

As my aunt talked, there was a quiet reverence around our kitchen table. We were all pondering this information. Even my vocal Grandma was silent. We didn't have many questions to ask, for we knew so little about God—only the small bits Grandma had gleaned from her visits to the church.

My aunt continued to visit us many times, and each time she told us a little bit more. At last, she invited us to accept Jesus' gift of salvation. "This is different than having a religion," Aunt Ilonka explained. "We need to accept what Jesus has already done for us. We call this grace: God's unmerited favor. The Bible says, 'It is by grace you have been saved, through faith—and this is not from yourselves, it is the gift of God—not by works, so that no one can boast.'"[2]

Our whole family decided to become followers of Jesus when I was nine years old.

One afternoon, I couldn't shake the feeling that I needed to do something more with my newfound faith. So I slipped away into a room by myself and prayed: "God, I want You to know that I love You." Suddenly I began to praise God in a language that I did not understand.

When I saw my mother and grandmother standing by the door with tears rolling down their cheeks, Grandma turned to my mother and said, "I wish I could be like her. That child has been touched by the Holy Spirit in a special way."

For me, that was only the beginning of my relationship with Jesus, my Savior. That habit of talking to God alone became an integral part of my life. I could tell God about all my joy and also my disappointments. No longer did I need to tell my stories to my cornhusk dolls. Jesus was a much better listener. But what surprised me most was that He seemed to also talk to my heart.

Little did I know how special—and critical—these soul conversations with God would become.

THESE SHOES WERE MADE FOR WALKIN'

Grandpa had taught me to walk when I was little.
Now he was teaching me the first steps
in the Christian walk.

After I decided to turn my life over to Christ, Grandpa, who had always been very special to me, began to read to me from his big black book, the Bible. My mom told me how Grandpa had taught me to walk with our shaggy dog's help when I was little. Now he was teaching me the first steps in the Christian walk.

I loved these special times with Grandpa a lot! I would sit under the table and stroke my pet cat and listen to Grandpa's big booming voice. Although I loved to hear him read, I have to admit that many times I did not understand what he was reading. There were so many concepts that seemed too deep for my reasoning at the time. I grasped the general sense of what he was reading. His words and the love in his voice as he read have stayed with me to this day.

Grandpa was in his seventies when he finally made peace with God and with others. When he became a Christian, that significant, life-transforming event took away any uncertainty Grandpa had about the future. He always lived out his faith before others, talking about Jesus even amid a communistic philosophy that didn't acknowledge God's existence.

Grandpa's zest for telling people about his Savior shone through in everything he did.

Grandpa had been sick in bed all week, growing weaker every day. But he had pushed our worries aside. "I don't need to see a doctor," he kept telling us. "I am just old and weak, and soon I will go to heaven to be with Jesus."

One afternoon as I came home, I saw most of the family crowding around Grandpa's bedside. Some of the grown-ups were talking; others were praying. I began to pray silently for my grandpa. My heart ached at seeing him so weak.

Then, all of a sudden, my beloved grandpa lifted his hands toward the ceiling. He smiled widely and mumbled joyfully, "Oh, they are coming for me!"

"Who is coming for you?" my grandmother asked with a trembling voice. "The angels?"

Grandpa didn't answer. He merely smiled once more. His face transformed with an expression of wonder. Then he stopped breathing.

Grandma reached over, closed his eyes, then sat holding his hand.

It was my first encounter with death, and I was stunned by its finality. I could hardly believe my grandpa was gone.

We all cried that day, but not without hope. Grandpa had told us, over and over, that soon he was going to heaven. He always said it with a ring in his voice as if he were anticipating the reunion with Jesus.

In the days to come, I would miss my grandpa fiercely. But I knew that someday I would join him in heaven because I, too, had chosen to accept Jesus in my heart and follow Him.

When I was fifteen years old, I had my own "almost" encounter with heaven. One evening, as I was working at home, a terrible pain stabbed my right side. I continued working despite the pain, but finally, I went to bed. All night long, I lay awake in terrible agony.

In the morning, my sister Rosie took me to the doctor. (In those days, you didn't go to the doctor unless you were ill.) Alarmed, he called the ambulance, and they took me to the hospital in Subotica. Since my twin sisters, Erika and Valerija, were only a few months old, my mother stayed at home with them and my two younger sisters: Maria, age nine, and Martha, age seven.

Once I was at the hospital, the doctor told my sister that I had a ruptured appendix. They needed to operate right away. I was terrified. *How could this be happening? And why?*

After the operation, they wheeled me into a four-bed room. When I woke up, I was in such intense pain that I barely had enough strength to open my eyes. My mouth was so dry that my tongue felt swollen. I overheard a patient in the bed next to mine say to her visitor, "She had surgery on her appendix. They aren't sure if she'll make it."

"Too bad," the visitor replied. "She's such a beautiful girl!"

I realized they were talking about me.

Complications followed, including inflammation. Finally, after two long weeks in the hospital, the doctor said I was ready to go home. My father arrived with a horse-drawn carriage to pick me up. On the long, rough road home, I felt every painful bump. The pain continued, so acute that my mother stayed by my side all night long.

In the morning, she sent my father to call the pastor to bring me my "last communion." They were sure I was going to die.

The pastor read 1 Corinthians 11:23-26 about the Lord's Supper and prayed a blessing over me.

As I lay quietly, I heard faint whispers: "It's just a matter of time, and she will die."

I closed my eyes and fell into a deep sleep.

The next morning, I awoke. I was so disappointed that I wasn't in heaven with Grandpa. I'd fallen asleep after making my peace with death the night before. And here I was in the morning—very much alive!

None of us knew what happened during the night, but something did. I slowly began to feel better and was even able to eat some broth. It was beautiful to see my family's somber mood turn to grateful delight.

A few days later, some women met for prayer at our house. (We had registered our home with the communist government as a place where more than one family met for prayer.) I felt strong enough to join them.

As we were praying, a very old woman announced in amazement, "I see two people wearing white garments. They are standing beside Elizabeth and holding a crown above her head. The crown is woven out of ripe wheat like at harvest time."

The room stilled. I felt a holy presence in the room. *Were those the angels? Was it a message about me? Would I be a part of some future harvest?*

Nobody elaborated more on that statement; no one seemed to know what the vision meant. But I remembered it for many decades to come.

Maybe God saved my life for a reason, I thought. *In that case, what is my life's purpose? What does God have in mind for me?*

DANCING SHOES AND DRESSMAKING

I started to design and sew dresses.
It sure beat working in the fields.

Since I couldn't go back to school, my mother decided I should learn a trade. She wanted me to become a seamstress. I wasn't tending the cows anymore, but I still worked in the fields. Since I wasn't a robust person, I often got sick from hard work all day.

My father agreed with my mother's idea. He saw that I wasn't as strong as my older sister, Rosie. Besides, the concept of me becoming a seamstress fit nicely with his idea of what a woman should be.

Becoming a seamstress suited me also. *It sure beats working in the fields,* I thought. Besides, it would take my mind off what I thought of as "my ruined future."

And so, at the age of thirteen, I started to design and sew dresses, mostly for my sisters.

My teacher praised my work. "You have a natural talent for this!"

I grew excited. *If I can't go to school, dressmaking is second best. Maybe I do have some talent.*

One day, a woman from my hometown who had seen my work asked if I would design a dress for her. She described how she wanted it to be: a fitted waist, short sleeves, and a white belt that would accent her slim figure. My hands trembled as I picked up the beautiful material and held the scissors to it. One wrong cut and her puffed sleeves would be flat as a pancake. There was not enough material to try again.

"Please, God, help me!" I prayed. "I didn't know this would be so hard!"

I took a breath, then started to snip away at the material, praying all the while. Fortunately, God answered my prayers. All my cuts were perfect!

A week later, I finished the project. When the woman came to pick up her dress, she was so satisfied that she handed me more money than I asked. I ran into the kitchen, where my mother was stirring the soup, and showed her the money.

"Mother, look!" I exclaimed. "On Sunday, I will give all this money to God!"

She raised an eyebrow. "Elizabeth, you don't need to give it all—only ten percent." But I felt so delighted at the very first pay that I wanted to give it all to God. Not knowing it, I acted on Proverbs 3:9, which says, "Honor the Lord with your wealth, with the firstfruits of all your crops." That money was my first crop, and I gave all of it joyfully, willingly, to the Lord.

My gift of designing and sewing turned out to be a tremendous blessing for many years to come. Over time I enjoyed dressing up the town's girls with stylish and inventive new fashions. I had more work than I could handle, and I worked long into the night.

When I turned sixteen, what appealed to me most was beauty and fashion: nice clothes, stylish shoes, and unique purses. Since I knew how to sew and design, I could afford to wear fashionable clothes that cost me little money. All it took was creativity.

On summer Sunday afternoons and evenings, my friends and I would often gather around a lake just to hang out. One afternoon, two young men—Tamas and Tibor—joined us. In their mid-twenties, they had just moved to our town because of their jobs. They were handsome and friendly enough, but we shared very different values.

After my grandfather had died, and I'd entered my teen years, my values had started to change. I thought less about my relationship with God and more about what I wanted to do with friends. *What had happened to the girl who was so elated at her first pay that she wanted to give it all to God?*

I stopped listening to those little nudges from God and got in big trouble.

MUDDY SHOES AND WRONG FRIENDS

"Keep this top-secret," he said.
"We could escape...."

After a couple of months, Tamas had a plan. I was as eager to hear about it as he was to tell us. My friends gathered, too, to listen to the exciting news.

"Keep this top-secret," he said. "You've heard Tibor and me talking about Western Europe and the opportunities people have there to get ahead."

My friends and I nodded. We knew this was true, for Margit, a nearby town friend, had married an American. Now she sent parcels home to Yugoslavia to help her family; her sisters' beautiful clothes made us all envious.

"Well," Tamas said slowly and dramatically, "we could escape."

We stared at him. Our imaginations fired up. We would gain so much if we escaped from Yugoslavia into Austria! We could study and work and make money and buy whatever we wanted. From that day on, my friends and I could talk about nothing else. I began to imagine what it would be like to live in a free country. Maybe I could even pursue my studies. I could make money and send lovely parcels home as my friend did.

Tamas and his friend talked passionately about how we'd cross the northern border of Yugoslavia into Austria. "We'll meet by the water tower," he told us. "Then we'll take the night train to Slovenia. There we will climb the Alps between the two countries and cross the border."

The idea was scintillating as the plan unfolded. My heart pounded with excitement—and fear.

I was thrilled with the thought of venturing out into the world, but I wondered, *Can I leave my family like that?* But, if I stayed in Yugoslavia, what future did I have? My father had strictly forbidden me to continue in school. *I could sew and design dresses anywhere. Why not in a country where I would be free?*

A tingle passed through me as I thought about what my life could be. Yes, I'd miss my family, but I hoped my friends would help me in the "new world"—especially since, at age sixteen, going on seventeen, I was the youngest in the group.

We began to make our plans. All my group of friends committed to going. We would leave in the fall of 1963. I kept the plan a secret from my family. I did not share it with my mother since I was unsure how she'd react, and I was afraid she might not keep it a secret. The only person I told was my married sister Rosie, who lived in another village. I often rode my bicycle to clean her house because she was very busy with her two children.

As we were dusting furniture one day, I leaned toward her. "Rosie, I have something to share with you."

She stopped her dusting and looked at me.

"Some of us are going to escape to Austria," I said breathlessly.

When she didn't protest, I went on to embellish all the freedoms I imagined myself enjoying—religious freedom, exciting work, and maybe even school. I dreamed aloud about the life I would make for myself on the other side of the border; how I would send parcels home to help my mother and father. I told her enthusiastically what a great help this would be for my mother, with her little twins Erika and Valerija.

Rosie was speechless. By now, she'd had to sit down to catch her breath from the shock of my news. After a while of studying me, though, she said quietly, "I'm surprised, but I want to support you in your decision."

When we said good-bye that day, she held me tight. Her tears dampened my dress. "I promise I will explain everything to my mother and father when you're gone," she said. "They know how important freedom is for your future. They will miss you, but they will be excited about your future in the West. I mean, who wouldn't want to go there?"

I cried, too, wondering if it was the last time I would embrace my sister.

Several days later, the departure time finally came. We had agreed to meet in the early afternoon by the water tower, a few kilometers away. From there, we would take the train and travel across Yugoslavia (now Slovenia) to the last town before the border. From there, we would climb the mountains at nightfall. Then, early in the morning, while it was still dark, we would sneak past the guards and cross the border into Austria.

But when I arrived at the water tower, only Tamas was there.

"Where is everybody?" I asked.

"They all chickened out!" he said in an irritated voice.

I wondered for an instant what had happened to my friends. *If they had decided not to go, why had nobody told me?*

"Do you still want to go?" he asked.

I felt very uneasy. From somewhere inside, a warning signal went off, telling me, *Don't go!* But I wanted to appear courageous to Tamas. After all, we'd spent so much time planning for this adventure.

I repositioned my fingers tightly around the handle of my small bag and nodded.

"Okay, let's go then," he said, turning toward the train station.

With each step, I tried to muster up the courage, even though I kept feeling uneasy. In silence, we boarded a train heading north toward the foothills of the Austrian Alps. As the doors of the train shut and the train began to move, I felt captured.

This is it, I thought. *Now you cannot go back.* After eight or ten hours on the train, I found it impossible to sleep. We finally arrived in Slovenia. After leaving the train, we headed toward the forest. As we started to climb the mountain, the night was so cold. It was raining, and the trek through the night seemed endless. I thought we would never make it. I was exhausted, and Tamas walked on, never stopping.

The next morning at dawn, we crossed the border between Yugoslavia and Austria into freedom. My dream, at last, was coming true. We had made it!

But my joy was short-lived.

"Give me all your money," Tamas demanded. "We need to exchange it for Austrian shillings, and I will keep it safe for you."

I dug into my bag and pulled out my money—and handed it to him.

Then we started to walk toward the first Austrian village. It took us a while to get there. I was so exhausted after the sleepless night, the trek over the mountains, and the fear of getting through the border that I could hardly put one foot in front of another.

As night fell, we finally entered a small hostel. I didn't speak German. Tamas, with his broken German, made all the arrangements.

I saw the hostel manager give him a key.

Suddenly I felt like a bird caught in a cage, flapping its wings wildly.

That night, Tamas robbed me of my most treasured gift—my purity, the very thing that I had cherished my entire life as a gift to a future husband.

Why did I let this happen to me? I kept condemning myself for trusting him. *I should have known better.*

As much as I wanted to imagine this was all a bad dream, I knew it was real. Deep sadness overcame me.

Throughout that very long, sleepless night, the sadness switched multiple times to anger, mixed with depression, and back to denial again. As hard as I tried, I could not wish the events of the past twenty-four hours away. I remained curled in a ball at the edge of the bed, amidst wet clothes and muddy shoes, and now a white bed sheet soiled.

I did not want to live.

ELIZABETH MITTELSTAEDT

FUNERAL SHOES AND
THE DEATH OF A DREAM

I wanted to kick him, to fight him,
to make him hurt for what he had done to me.
But I had no energy to say or do anything.

The next morning after my endless night, Tamas said casually, "Let's go for breakfast."

But I refused, and he went by himself. While he was away, I got out of bed and looked at my reflection in the mirror. It was a reflection of shame and regret. I felt like part of me had died.

I stepped to the window and saw the lush, green hills of freedom. Then a taunting voice spoke: "You'd be better off dead than alive."

I found myself agreeing.

The voice kept teasing and toying with me: "Why don't you end it all?"

Then, something deep within me uttered a simple, silent cry: "God, please help!"

During that time, when Tamas was gone, I wrestled with myself.

Strangely, the story of Snow White popped into my mind. She was offered a golden apple that looked delicious on the surface but turned out to be poisonous. I'd been offered the golden apple of freedom and hadn't looked carefully enough for the poison.

Yes, I'd made the wrong choice to trust a man who didn't share the same values I'd grown up with. But now, all I wished was that, like Snow White, I could fall asleep for a very long time.

Then another memory flooded my mind. It was a memory of a long-buried time when my cousin had sexually abused me. That had not been the result of making the wrong choice.

I was only four years old when a distant cousin came to visit us. Mother had left the house to milk the cows, and none of my sisters were at home, so I was alone with him. Suddenly...

"Don't be afraid," he said.

But I was terrified.

Suddenly, we heard footsteps approaching, and he quickly pulled his pants back up. "Don't you dare tell anyone about this," he hissed. When my mother entered with a full pail of milk, he acted as if nothing had happened.

But my mother must have seen the distress in my eyes. "What's wrong, Elizabeth?" she asked me.

"Nothing," I said. "I don't feel well. I want to go to sleep."

Confusion and sadness overwhelmed me. I made myself bury the ugly incident and never told anyone about it.

When Tamas returned from breakfast and saw that I was still distraught, he said, "We'll go to the police headquarters. We need to make a petition for political asylum."

I simply nodded.

The rest of that day is only a haze in my memory.

I was unnerved by the cold, impersonal police building. But the Austrian policeman was friendly.

"We'd like to apply for political asylum," Tamas said, handing the man his papers. He was speaking in German, so I couldn't understand what he was saying. But I observed and copied what he was doing. I opened my bag and pulled out my papers.

But by the expression on Tamas' face, I could tell he wasn't happy with what the police officer told him. He shook his head and replied something back to the officer.

The officer now looked at me and said something, but I just stared at him, not knowing what he was telling me to do. He moved around the counter and, taking my arm, led me down a corridor away from Tamas.

My heart began to pound. *Where was he taking me?*

The police officer kept explaining something to me, but it was all garbled since I didn't understand the language. At last, he motioned for me to get into a police car and then drove me down the street.

Where are we going? I wondered. I was terrified.

In front of a tall, forbidding building, we stopped. We entered and proceeded down a hall filled with jail cells. I watched in disbelief as the guard took out a key, opened the door, and ushered me inside. I stepped inside the small, cramped space, which held one cot, a sink, and a toilet.

The heavy door shut with the clank of a metal lock clicking tight.

I had no idea why I was locked up or how long I would be there.

Exhausted, hot tears began to stream down my face. I was so afraid that I curled onto the lumpy, hard bed and cried myself to sleep.

That was a Thursday. For the next six days, I remained in that cell. I cried a lot and, from time to time, managed to sleep a little. Three times a day, the guards handed me food through a tiny window. Even though they were friendly, I became more and more afraid. *What would happen to me?*

Finally, an officer led me outside to a small police van and motioned for me to get in. I squeezed in with about ten other foreigners—folks like me seeking refuge in Austria. Then they told us to get on a bus, and we were all taken to a hearing. Tamas was there, too. He had been taken to another prison.

After the hearing, they locked Tamas up again. I could move about freely. They deported him back to Yugoslavia. I wondered, *Had the police found something in his records? And what will happen to me?*

A few weeks later, after staying at a refugee camp, I was scheduled for another hearing by the Austrian government. Through an interpreter, the Austrian government agent asked me, "Where would you like to go?"

That choice was easy. "America or Germany!" I said.

Then I heard the news: "But only Australia is currently receiving refugees."

So they assigned me to that continent. In the days to follow, I was very restless. I couldn't imagine going to Australia—the end of the world, as far as I was concerned.

In my confusion, I did not know what to do. By then, all I could think of was home and my family. I was hurting so badly.

I waited a few more days.

Then, at last, I walked into the Yugoslav embassy in Vienna and announced, "I want to go home to Yugoslavia."

The officer gave me a big grin. "Okay," he said as he issued me a train ticket.

By requesting to leave the West and return to the East, I had proved his point: life was better in a communist country. I grabbed my small traveling bag and walked to the train station.

So there I sat, in a fresh change of clothes, on a train heading east, back to Yugoslavia. I wasn't sure if life would ever be the same. All I knew was that my dream of freedom had been a farce.

CEMENT-LOGGED SHOES AND MY TRIP HOME

No one ever said a word about my trip to the West.
We all just carried on as if nothing had happened.

Every kilometer of the train ride home was pure agony. Each rotation of the wheels over the tracks sounded like the years of my young life ticking away. Even though I was exhausted, I could not stop replaying the events of the last few weeks.

The walk from the train station to my parents' home seemed like forever. I felt like I was wearing cement-logged shoes. I wanted to disappear into the shadows—hoping no one would see me.

Although I was afraid of my actions' consequences, never was I more grateful to look down and have that familiar dust of my hometown under my feet again.

As I turned onto our street, I paused. I had such mixed feelings: fear about my family's response, embarrassment that my dreams had amounted to nothing, guilt that I'd caused my parents anguish, and anger that things had turned out the way they did.

At last, I made my decision. *I don't care about the consequences,* I thought. *I want to be home again.*

When I reached my house, my mother already stood at the door. She must have seen me coming somehow. A split second later, she rushed to hug me for several minutes. Then she pulled back, and with tears in her eyes, leaned toward me, studying my sullen face. My father and I had a hard time looking at each other. I knew he must have been as ashamed and unsure of what to do with me as I was with myself.

It was tough to start a conversation. Each of us waited for the other to begin to speak.

By this time, I was sure my parents already knew that it was not a group escape.

Later my parents told me they knew Tamas had returned—without me—and knew that he took part in some illegal activities. They'd assumed then that I'd stayed in the West and made a life for myself there. I didn't know until much later that, as much as they missed me, my parents were sad I had given up my future in the West to return to Yugoslavia.

That's the way it felt to be back home—awkward. All my friends knew, of course, that I had taken off with Tamas. Though I think most of them were initially envious of my bravery, now I was sure they considered me an even greater fool for returning home. But no one ever said a word about my trip to the West—or why they hadn't shown up that day at the water tower. We all just carried on as if nothing had happened, even though it was apparent to everyone that something had happened.

I tried hard to shove down the memory of that horrid first night in Austria, the supposed "land of freedom." I wanted to bury it so deep that the images would never again plague my memory. Sometimes shoving the feelings down worked. Other times trying to forget that event made the remembering even worse.

Many nights my pillow was wet with tears. My wounded soul was bleeding; the horror, at times, wouldn't stay hidden. I vacillated between guilt, self-condemnation, and anger. Had my natural curiosity about exploring the world beyond the boundaries of our little village pulled me into such a bad situation? Or had it been my choice of friends who cared nothing about God or my values? Or both?

It took many years to leave those cement-logged shoes behind, but it sure felt good when I did.

A couple of months after returning home, I realized I had not had my period. When I mentioned it to an older friend, she took me to a doctor.

When we arrived at the doctor's office, I sat nervously in the waiting room until a nurse called my name. I followed her down a hallway and into a small space. This bare room didn't look like a regular doctor's office to me. None of the ordinary doctor's instruments were in sight—just an examination table.

"Undress from the waist down, and then lie on the table," the nurse said as she turned out the lights and left the room. "The doctor will be right in."

"This might hurt a bit, but don't worry. You'll be fine," a deep voice said. The room was dark. I never saw the doctor's face.

Never before had a doctor examined this part of my body. Mother had never talked to me about sex, and we didn't learn anything about this subject in school either. So I had no idea what to expect. I was terrified.

Suddenly, I felt a searing pain as the doctor ripped something out of my body. Then, without another word, he left the room. He offered no explanation and no pain medication.

I knew something terrible had just happened. But what? I shakily got up off the table, got dressed, and headed back to the waiting room with terrible pain.

Later I asked my mother, "What the doctor did to me…is that killing a baby?"

My mother looked at me. "No! At conception, it's just a clump of blood. Only after three months does it become a baby." She explained that most women had this procedure done several times. "Otherwise, they'd end up having so many children, they wouldn't be able to care for them all," she explained.

Later, I learned that life begins at conception. I felt betrayed that nobody had told me the truth. I grieved desperately, knowing that I killed my baby. Intense waves of emotional and physical pain swept over me. One wrong choice—the escape—had brought about a second wrong choice—the abortion.

"Oh, God, please forgive me," I prayed.

I saw clearly how everyday choices could influence one's future.

The reality that I had let my baby die left a hole in my heart for years to come. Until God surprisingly redeemed even that cruel act by His unimaginable grace.

After a few months, I dared to go back to church. On the first Sunday, I stared down at my fashionable shoes. I could dress up my outside, but inside, I felt ugly.

Despite what I had done, I longed to have fellowship with other believers once again.

The pastor preached a sermon on the parable Jesus told of the prodigal son returning home to his father. He read from the Gospel of Luke: "…The son said to him, 'Father, I have sinned against heaven and against you. I am no longer worthy to be called your son.' But the father said to his servants, 'Quick! Bring the best robe and put it on him. Put a ring on his finger and sandals on his feet. Bring the fattened calf and kill it. Let's have a feast and celebrate.'"[3]

As the pastor read and preached about the lost son, I watched my inner movie and titled it, *The Lost Daughter*. Like the prodigal son, I had a decision to make: would I return to my heavenly Father or continue to live as if He didn't exist?

I gathered my courage and prayed silently, "Father in heaven, I took my life into my own hands and ran away. And I paid a high price for it. It is so painful to revisit these places of shame again and again. I don't want to feel the hurt anymore. Will you help me?"

Several weeks later, as I was taking communion, I checked my own heart. Yes, there was not only deep pain dwelling there but also resentment and unforgiveness. I knew that in the Lord's Prayer, Jesus taught His disciples to pray, "Forgive us our sins, as we have forgiven those who sin against us."[4]

I was so overwhelmed by Jesus' suffering. He had done that to pay for my sins, to reconcile me to God, so that I could enjoy our fellowship again.

"I want to forgive, yet the pain is so great," I prayed. "Please, Holy Spirit, help me. I can't do this in my strength."

ELIZABETH MITTELSTAEDT

I sensed a gentle whisper: "You're right. You cannot forgive on your own. But I will help you."

I inhaled deeply, again summoning my courage. "Lord Jesus, I choose to forgive, even though I don't feel like it."

Voicing my forgiveness allowed me to begin releasing the burden of feeling responsible for fixing it. By saying, "Forgive Tamas, Lord," I was letting God be the one to deal with him.

I wish I could say I experienced an immediate sense of relief that day. But that would be far from the truth. My heart was still tender from the wounds, and the wounds would need time to heal.

At times I still found it difficult to shake the "victim" identity. Far too often, I fell into false guilt, believing that I deserved all this shame, blame, and disapproval. I know now that was a lie of Satan to keep me mired in the hell of self-condemnation. Satan wanted me to believe that Jesus' love and forgiveness, His death and resurrection weren't enough to cover my sins.

I had to choose consciously to believe the truth, even though my feelings spoke otherwise. At such times, when guilt overwhelmed my soul, I'd cry out, "Lord, I do believe Your forgiveness is enough. And Lord Jesus, heal me! Heal my mind, my spirit, and my emotions!"

Little by little, the healing came. When I chose to extend forgiveness and mercy to Tamas, he no longer controlled my present or future. Yes, he had influenced my past and inflicted physical, mental, and emotional pain upon me that I would never forget. But when I made the gut-wrenching decision to forgive him, my spirit was freed to walk, unhampered, into my future.

As time went on, I became less consumed with my past struggles and more compelled to do whatever it would take to find freedom in Christ. I determined that I would embrace all that God had for me. I would not give any foothold to Satan by harboring unforgiveness.

I also had to choose to forgive myself. Yes, I had made bad choices. I had not chosen good friends.

That day, when I forgave myself, I realized I needed to leave my story of regret behind me.

Though I didn't realize it until much later, forgiving Tamas and forgiving myself were two defining moments in my life because my desperate need for God's grace and forgiveness opened the door to greater intimacy with Him.

Being able to let go of a "victim" mentality demanding either pity or penance gave me the ability to begin healing. It's when you can un-clench your fingers to let go of the ball of pain that you can open your hand to receive God's gift of mercy and forgiveness.

The memory of that painful experience will always remain with me, but that day I glimpsed and began to experience true freedom in both heart and mind. Accepting God's forgiveness, forgiving others, and forgiving myself was a major faith-leap forward.

SERVANT SHOES AND A SERVING HEART

Five little words transformed my thinking.

My desire to serve God grew as I began to live in the light of His redemption.

As I read my Bible in Hebrews 11, Gods' Hall of Fame, I found Rahab, a harlot between these greats. Jesus came from this genealogy! These greats were all human, yet God used them. Each had a story to tell of what God had done in their lives.

The truth of God using flawed people struck home. *In that case, I also have a story to tell to others*, I thought. *Help me, Lord Jesus, not to waste my hard-fought freedom story, either.*

My passion for God kept growing.

During that time in my life, I discovered that when we ask God for help, He usually responds with only five little words: "I will be with you."

I will be with you. Not a pep talk to make me feel better about myself or to improve my confidence. Not an elaborate plan that details every step, nor a self-help guide to make me a better Christian. Just the sweet assurance that relationally God will never leave me, nor forsake me.

I will be with you. I took the plunge of faith—and dared to believe that I could hang my life on those five words.

A year later, I went to Pastor Rac, who had seen me through so many stages in my walk of faith, and asked, "Is there anything I can do in the church?"

My heart desired to serve God in whatever way I could.

He rubbed his chin, then told me the names of a few older ladies. "They are sick and have no family," he said. "You could visit them and help them in whatever way they need you."

Okay, I thought. *I can do this.*

So twice a week, on my way home from my work as a seamstress, I stopped by their houses and helped with whatever they asked me to do.

Aunt Kis was so sick and overweight that she could barely get up. When I arrived at her house, she often asked me to cook for her or go shopping. But one day, she asked me if I would bathe her. I'm sure my wide-eyed surprise betrayed how uneasy I felt. I'm also sure it was just as humbling for her to ask me as it was for me to undertake this task for her.

While the water was heating, I helped Aunt Kis undress. I was so nervous. It was a far cry from dressing and undressing my corncob dolls when I was a child.

Every time I visited the older women from my church, they were so grateful. "Jesus will bless you for this," one of them would say as she grasped my hand. "He will bless you for the goodness you are showing to me."

I did not realize until later that my ministry began by washing old ladies' feet. And then I marveled, for I remembered that Jesus, on the last night before His death, washed the disciples' dirty feet.

The following year I found an excellent job in the city sewing fine clothes for export. Pastor Rac passed away, and a new pastor, Mr. Sabo, stepped into his shoes.

Although I missed my beloved pastor, who had done so much to set my feet on a godly path again, I knew that God would keep His hand on me. He would never leave me. This time His "I will be with you" brought an invitation from Mr. Sabo's family to live with them so I wouldn't have to travel into the city each day from the village.

I had just turned eighteen years old—and felt like I had already experienced enough grief and grace for a lifetime.

ELIZABETH MITTELSTAEDT

Sister Arnold, an eighty-year-old widowed woman, led the children's ministry in our church. I joined her in teaching the children. It was such a delight to see how Sister Arnold loved children! She always had tender words and a welcoming smile for each one of them. And the kids loved her, too.

There was no children's material at the time, so Sister Arnold wrote her own stories. She reminded me a bit of my grandmother, who'd entertained me with stories. Similarly, each of her stories helped the children understand specific values and virtues that taught them about loving Jesus and loving others.

Sister Arnold's affection for children also passed on to me. I loved the children and often saved what little money I earned from sewing to buy sweets for them. Since their parents could not afford to buy candy, this was a special treat for them. I want to think it was my marvelous storytelling that caused the Sunday school to grow, but perhaps it was the combination of sweet candies with sweet stories in tandem with precious children learning the sweet truths about God.

When I was thirteen, they shattered my dream to become a teacher. But now, to my amazement, I was teaching children life's most important lessons! Indeed, God does redeem lives and circumstances. I am living proof.

The love I received from serving elderly ladies and children fulfilled me immensely. A year or two before this, I couldn't have dreamed that I would be this happy again. Having tasted the pleasure of working for God, I craved even more. I wanted to be available for whatever job He had in store for me. I couldn't get over it: God was using me.

What I had experienced in the past few years was so remarkable. I had wanted freedom, crossing the border into Austria. Instead, God granted me the privilege of forgiveness and service. He was so good, withholding just punishment and replacing it with undeserved grace. How I agreed with David, the psalmist of old: "God's a safe-house for the battered, a sanctuary during bad times. The moment you arrive, you relax; you're never sorry you knocked."[5]

From time to time, it passed through my mind how different my life might have been if I could have pursued my education. But it was time to let that dream go, to forget what was behind me, and press on, asking God for a new dream.

A WALK IN THE CLOUDS

I had a choice to make.
Would I step back into what was familiar—
or continue forward in faith?

That summer of my eighteenth year, our youth group visited a church in another city for a week of collaborative activities. During that week, a young man caught my eye. He seemed to notice me, too. As I became better acquainted with him, he seemed so different from the other guys—not only was he attractive, but he had a deep love for God and wanted to serve Him. He was gentle and kind and loved people, especially children and seniors. I was drawn to him by his character, his faith, and his love for God.

We saw each other during special church meetings. By the way he looked at me and made sure to be around me, I began to realize that he liked me too. All of a sudden, I felt as if I were taking a walk in the clouds.

Maybe he was my first real love. I don't know. In my early teen years, I had felt fluttering with the neighbor boy, Beni, but this was different.

This young man's coming into my life felt like spring rain that gently quenches the thirst of parched land. I started dreaming: *Lord, is he the one? Can I team up with him and support him in his calling? Could we work together to make a life—and a difference for You?*

Half a year later, he invited me to meet his parents. I was thrilled! After all the introductions, it seemed I had been "approved" by his family. He and I went for a walk in the evening. Clouds rolled in from the west, a strong wind began blustering, and a thunderstorm appeared to be forming, but we walked on, hand in hand.

Then, out of the blue, he asked me, "Have you had sexual relations with a man?"

The question surprised me, but I could understand why he was asking. No doubt, he had heard about my background—about the mysterious missing weeks during my sixteenth year.

Lying didn't even enter my mind. I would trust God with the results. So, without hesitation, I answered: "Yes."

I was glad it was already dark, and he could not see my face. My mind froze with the reality of what had happened to me in that horrific period in my life. I just answered, "Yes." I didn't want to tell my story. I didn't want to explain, for that would mean reliving that experience all over again.

After that, he grew quiet. He didn't ask me any other questions, and I didn't make any comments. He silently escorted me back to my friend's house, where I was staying. As we neared the house, it started to rain, and we both got drenched.

Once in front of the door, he politely said good night. That was all. No more.

And then he left.

That was our last walk together.

My walk in the clouds had been brief. It had set up longing for a home and family of my own. Now the familiar feelings of shame and rejection tried to creep back into my soul.

For a while, I let them. I wallowed in them.

After weeks of sadness, I knew I had a choice to make. Would I step back into what was familiar—the doubts, the shame, the guilt, the bitterness—or continue forward in faith, trusting that God knew what's best for my welfare?

So I prayed, "Yes, Lord, I am disappointed and hurt by his rejection. But who knows what You have reserved for me down the road? Whom are You keeping just for me? I choose to trust You."

I crumpled to my knees on the carpet, face down, crying, until I regained the strength to get back up. As I did, I felt God's love surround me, giving me the courage to go on.

That day I learned how vital my heart is—as the common ground of where God and I meet. It's the place where faith and love take root, where hope blossoms. It is my greatest gift from God, and I have a responsibility to protect it. Like Proverbs says, "Above all else, guard your heart, for everything you do flows from it."[6]

That day I allowed God to replace the hurt in my heart with hope—a hope that would blossom in a surprising form years down the road.

Then I met Olga Olsson.

Olga was tall and slim and had a smattering of gray sprinkled throughout her hair. She was a Swedish-American Assemblies of God missionary who served in Germany and "just happened" to be visiting our church.

Sitting on a hard, wooden bench without a back, I barely noticed my discomfort because I was so engrossed in how she spoke about God's Word. As a woman, she was allowed to speak at my church because she was a missionary and a Bible School teacher.

Olga talked passionately about how God had used women in the Bible. As Olga shared what God was doing in and through her own life, I whispered to God, "In case You ever need another woman like Olga, I sure would love to be that woman!"

I believe that was the moment of my calling into ministry. *Yes, yes,* my heart kept saying, *I want to serve God like that!* I set my life purpose that day.

Perhaps Olga saw the desire on my face as she was speaking through an interpreter. When she finished, I rushed over to her to thank her for her message. She smiled and said, "Do you truly desire to serve God?"

"Yes," I said.

She smiled. "You know, there's a college in Germany where you can get training in both Bible and practical ministry. If you're interested, I can help you to go."

I couldn't believe what she was telling me. *Who am I? I am not worthy of this honor.*

I spoke to my parents about it.

My mother was thrilled. "I know your heart's deepest desire has always been to continue your education," she said. "Your dad did not let you go on to study because of the financial cost. But I also had a reason: I knew if you accepted a government scholarship, you would have had to become a member of the communist party. They would have indoctrinated you with their ideology, their plan for your life."

I was stunned. I had never stopped to consider the possibility of reasons other than my father's stubborn "Nem."

As my mother spoke, I began to see God's plan unfolding. God had been at work all the time, behind the scenes of my life. *What else might He be doing that I was unaware of?*

"As difficult as it was for you," my mother continued, "I felt God had His hand upon you even before you were born. Did you know He protected you when I was pregnant? I was supposed to abort you."

I blinked. No, I'd never heard that story before.

"When I was carrying you, I suffered from diphtheria. There was no medicine then, and my life, as well as yours, was in danger. Many people wanted me to abort you. 'Save your own life,' they said. But I thought, 'I don't have much chance to live through it myself. So no, then we'll die together.'"

At that moment, I understood much more about my mother, and I was deeply grateful to her. Abortion was common in Eastern Europe, and many women had several abortions in their lifetime. Yet my mother had risked her life for me!

Soon I received a letter from a hotel in Frankfurt, Germany, guaranteeing a place for me to live and work. Along with it came legal permission to enter the country of Germany.

About eight months later, in January 1968, it was time to leave. I packed some new dresses that I had recently sewn and gathered a few other personal items. I was so eager to go, for it meant pursuing my long-held dream. As I said good-bye to my family and friends, though, sadness crept in. I didn't know if I would ever see them again. I didn't know if the political situation would worsen as it had when the Berlin Wall went up, separating families between East and West Germany.

Despite all these questions, though, I was ready and willing to take the risk. On the evening before I was to leave, Pastor Sabo advised me, "You better leave the country early in the morning…just in case the authorities change their minds. If they do, you'll be long gone."

As I lay in bed that night, I remembered how I'd put all the broken pieces of my life into God's hands. At the time, I had no idea how God would be putting them back together again. And now He was giving me a chance to go to Germany to study. *You are a good Father to me,* I thought.

Before the sun rose the next morning, Pastor and Mrs. Sabo helped me carry my suitcase to the train station. They traveled with me to Belgrade (about a four-hour ride). Before assisting me in boarding the international train for Germany, they prayed that God would bless and keep me. I gave them one last loving look and settled into my seat. As the train pulled away, I wondered what God would have in store for me on this new adventure.

During those last few years I lived in Yugoslavia, I faced deep disappointments, but as I left my home country, I was no longer drowning in hopelessness and despair. Nor was I excusing, rationalizing, or blaming circumstances or people anymore. I was thankful for God's grace and forgiveness, which I received not by feelings but by faith.

How glad I am to be back on track with you, God, I thought, as the train clattered toward its destination in the West. *Help me, in the future, to make good choices—choices that please you. Choices that move my life passionately toward Your purpose for me.*

GIVE-AWAY SHOES AND DAYS OF SPLENDOR

*Millions of questions about my new life
raced through my mind.*

I had never imagined myself back on the same train tracks, crossing
the exact border of Yugoslavia that I had traversed nearly five years
earlier. The giant Austrian mountains still looked as massive as they
did then, and the border guards carrying their rifles intimidated me.

Even though I had official papers granting permission to travel
and work in Germany, millions of questions about my new life raced
through my mind. *Would I make any friends? Would I be able to learn a
foreign language? Would I survive at college?*

Out the window, a pure-white blanket of snow covered the Austrian countryside. With church steeples rising high into the sky, the
villages were like paintings I imagined from a fairytale. Everything
seemed so idyllic, almost surreal. I began to think about my past.
What healing the last five years had brought to my soul! Only God's
generous kindness and the distance of time had enabled me to have the
courage to retrace these steps. I was so glad to be no longer stuck in a
prison of shame and unforgiveness.

How foolish I was when I took things into my own hands during
that first escape. If I had just waited for God's timing, I would have
avoided much pain for myself and others. *But thank You, God, for loving me anyway,* I prayed. *You're such a gracious God and loving Father. I
know You could have prevented what happened five years ago; I also know
it was not your perfect plan for me. I took a detour in life, thinking I knew
better. Still, it does not mean that You can't use what happened for good.*

I thought of a verse in the Bible that says, "You, LORD, you are our Father. We are the clay, you are the potter; we are all the work of your hand."[7] During the last few years, I had been on the potter's wheel. The shaping process was excruciating, but the pain was purposeful. I could already see that the pain of the reshaping was worth it all.

From the first moment I stepped off the train, the bustle of the big city of Frankfurt, Germany, energized me. Unlike the quaint villages in the Austrian Alps and my simple dusty-road village in Yugoslavia, Frankfurt was an expansive metropolis with tall buildings and a flurry of activity. Being there was like a dream: I was finally encountering the big West. It was a "real" world, a grown-up world. A world I had only heard and dreamed about.

Olga had arranged for two people to meet me at the train station to take me to my new "home"—a hotel where I would work as a maid in exchange for room and board. My wage would also help pay for college. I had sent a photo of myself and told them what train I would be arriving on.

I remember how the train was "swallowed" by the huge train station in Frankfurt. When I stepped out of the train with my one suitcase, I immediately saw a lady and a man smiling at me. So I met their eyes and walked toward them. They said something I did not understand, but I assumed it was "Welcome." I just smiled back. The young man politely took my suitcase. As we walked through this large international train station, I heard many different languages. I was also surprised to see so many dark-haired, dark-eyed people. Weren't all Germans blond-haired and blue-eyed?

The young man led us to a Volkswagen Beetle. After the three of us shoved into his little two-door car, he started up the motor. We twisted and turned our way through the streets of Frankfurt on our way to the hotel. By the daring manner in which our driver took turns, I wondered whether he was showing off. Every new sight delighted me. *Belgrade is a beautiful city,* I thought, *but this city has so many tall buildings, banks, and hotels. There must be many rich people living here.*

"Willkommen," the lady behind the reception desk said as I stepped through the main hotel door into a small lobby beautifully decorated with fresh flowers. Everything looked so clean and lovely!

I worked the next day, so the manager sent an Italian lady to give me instructions. She took me to one of the floors and showed me how to clean a room. Trying very hard to understand her instructions, I paid close attention to her gestures. Over time the cleaning of rooms, floors, and windows became routine. Although the days were long, I was grateful for the opportunity to work.

My goal was to study German in the evenings, but I was so exhausted that I fell asleep far too often. During the day, I worked with a maid from Italy who did not speak much more German than I, and what she did say was not correct grammar. So my learning of the German language was both slow-going and mediocre. I found little victories thrilling, such as buying bread and cheese at the market or asking for directions and understanding the responses. But most days, I felt clumsy and was humbled as I tried to interact with others in this new world.

Then my pastor wrote to tell me there was a question whether or not I would be allowed to study at college because some church leaders from Yugoslavia feared that I would inspire other women to follow in my footsteps. Disheartened by such news, I fell to my knees and cried out to God.

There were times when I was tempted to listen to Satan's lies: "You're not good enough. Your past has disqualified you. Women are supposed to be quiet."

But I could not forget how God had chosen Deborah, Esther, Lydia, and missionaries like Olga to do great things for Him. He had miraculously paved the way for me to be in Germany, and I was confident He would make His way.

During this challenging waiting time, I sometimes gave in to discouragement. *I should forget about college,* I thought. *It will be too difficult anyway.*

One evening, while thinking these unhappy thoughts, I knelt beside my bed and told God, "I will not get up from my knees until I hear from You. What is the right thing to do?" I did not want my feelings to guide me, but His perfect will.

Finally, after midnight, I heard God's whisper in my heart: "One day, when you stand before Me, you will not be accountable for what people say about you and want you to do. But you will be accountable for what I ask you to do."

I knew I had to pursue college.

Finally, the day came when the school president said to me, "Welcome to the school!" I was very excited and relieved to hear the news. Waiting on God had been worth it—it always is—for the timing was indeed right.

On the first day at college, I moved into a dorm room that I would share with two female students from Germany—Ursula and Inge. We became fast friends. They took me under their wings, helping me to learn German. Under their tutelage, I progressed much faster. I was so grateful to have patient people I could count on.

Each morning was filled with classes or work, with occasional lessons in the afternoons. I had to study more than the others because of the wide language gap. Somehow, through a lot of hard work and help from friends and gracious teachers, I passed the exams.

I was so happy to be back at college, even though it was difficult for me, especially the language.

Two of my teachers at the school were Paul and Gladys Williscroft. They had been Assemblies of God missionaries in Poland before World War II. After the war, they had moved to Germany to help at the college. Still, their heartbeat was for Eastern European countries. They were the greatest children's workers I had ever known. They took me under their wings, and, through their sensitive nature, they saw the many unspoken questions of my heart. Often I went with them to the church where Gladys taught children and was amazed at how she communicated the message so simply that the children could understand.

We spent many hours talking about life and hope—and the future and God.

Nine months later, all of my first-year classes and exams were behind me. I couldn't believe I had made it! The formal studies had stopped for the summer, yet they expected us to put head knowledge into practice by participating in a summer ministry internship. Every girl found a place to intern—except me.

What next, God? my soul cried out.

CHILD-SIZED SHOES, GIANT-SIZED FAITH

What I witnessed took my breath away.

One day Paul Williscroft suggested, "Why don't you go back home to Yugoslavia for the summer and start a children's camp? Later, we will come and help you."

The suggestion resounded within my heart. I loved working with children, and there was a great need for this ministry since the concept of a children's camp was yet unheard of in communist countries. Once again, obstacles jumped into my view like bricks forming an insurmountable wall: *Would the communist government permit us to run a Christian camp? Where could we accommodate all the children? How would we pay? What teaching materials would we use?*

The questions were huge, but my passion for the project was greater. In January, when the Williscrofts and I had first brainstormed the idea, we had begun making plans. In February, I had written to Pastor Sabo about the project. He was excited. Since President Tito was now opening the border to the West, it was no problem for me to return to my homeland. The Williscrofts, as well, had no trouble getting visitor's visas.

Then the wait until June began.

In June, with faith and my packed bags in hand, I boarded a train heading east toward my homeland. The Williscrofts would join me in a few weeks.

As the train rolled toward Subotica, the city of my home church, I gazed across the flat landscape with only a few trees, thinking, *Hmm, this is not as green as Germany; it's much hotter and dryer here, but still, it feels good to come home.*

We settled on having the camp in Ada, a city about two hours from my hometown. We found a church there with a courtyard that could host sixty active children.

The first "brick in our insurmountable wall" was getting permission from the police. I found out nothing had changed one bit from my earlier years. Their power and control were still as daunting as ever. I asked some of the older ladies in my home church to fast and pray with me, with fear clutching my insides. We crafted a letter that asked permission to have a children's camp from Monday to Saturday.

A few days later, a reply came by mail refusing permission.

We continued our earnest prayer vigil and, a week later, we sent another request to the police. This time they approved it. We were so excited, praising God for answered prayer.

Not taking anything for granted, we held another prayer meeting before we continued with any more planning. Then we set our sights toward preparing for the camp. It had been no problem to get sixty kids together. After announcing it, the spots filled up quickly with children, many of whom had never been on vacation or away from home before.

The camp would be a week-long, and the children, ages seven to eleven. Paul and Gladys and I would be the teachers. I found it comical that I would now be a translator after all my language struggles of the past year.

Now we had our permission, much enthusiasm, and a clear purpose for the camp. It wasn't flashy—we just wanted to give the children a chance to play and laugh and tell them about Jesus. We wanted to show them how much God loves them and that the life He has for them is worth living. I had purchased some children's Bible materials in Germany using the money I saved from working at the hotel.

Everything seemed set—the permission, the materials, the teachers. But as the start of the camp drew near, Pastor Sabo asked me, "How will you feed all these children?"

God had already provided for that, too. When I returned home for the summer, my mother had given me money for shoes. *Why shoes?* I wondered. Was my mother thinking of the Scripture verse, "How beautiful...are the feet of those who bring good news?"[8] I knew my mother wouldn't mind me giving up buying shoes so the children at camp could have something to eat. So I used the money towards the price of buying a pig.

My aunt Giza and her husband were a dedicated couple who oversaw the kitchen with some other ladies' help. My aunt was a great cook, and before we knew it, our piggy had yielded enough meat to feed sixty children for a whole week. We were off to a good start.

We put up a big tent for the children to sleep in because we did not have a building large enough to hold them all. Since mattresses were unavailable, we piled straw on the floor and covered it with blankets. It was roughing it, but the kids loved the adventure. The children were so excited by this unique "sleepover" that they had difficulty sleeping the first night.

Bright and early, at five o'clock in the morning, I could see their heads poking out from underneath the tent. The camp had already started to wear me out—even before the first full day had begun! But it was worth it. When I opened the tent, the kids looked like little pigs all squished in together. It was great!

Breakfast consisted of bread, jam, and sometimes a piece of salami along with tea. Following this, there was a devotional time, then a Bible lesson. The afternoons were play time. We'd take the children for long walks into the forest or play around the camp area: ball games, rope jumping, and musical chairs.

Each evening, after dinner, we had a service with singing and Bible teaching. Then it was off to the tent for sleep. On the third night, we taught about the cross of Jesus and how He willingly chose to die a humiliating and painful death for each one of us. Many of the children were stirred by Jesus' love. We hadn't solicited their response; it just welled up from their tender hearts. They wept and prayed aloud. The camp staff was afraid even to move—we did not want to upset

God's deep work. We were utterly overwhelmed by the Holy Spirit's presence.

When I opened my eyes, I was shocked. All kinds of people, even gypsies and other children, were standing by the fence, looking at us. Somehow the Spirit of God touched those outside that courtyard.

The praying continued, and we finally decided that the children should get some rest. We would follow up with them in the morning. Trying to get sixty seven-to-eleven-year-olds to use one outhouse and get them ready for bed was like trying to corral wild ponies. Finally, about an hour later, I thought they had settled down.

Then I heard a noise.

Those little rascals! I thought. *How can they goof off after an evening like this?*

I followed the noise, expecting to have an unpleasant encounter like children fighting. What I witnessed took my breath away. Before me was a circle of boys kneeling and praying aloud for one another. They could not stop praying. They could not sleep.

I was so touched and humbled. I smiled, then let the children be. There would always be time for sleep. God was clearly at work.

The Holy Spirit surprised us; about twenty children surrendered their lives to Jesus that night, and most of the other children made the same decision throughout the week. The following day, some children gave testimony of what had happened to them. One eleven-year-old boy moved us to tears as he shared how he tried to take his own life a few weeks before because of a difficult family situation. But now, he knew God loved him and had saved him. "I will trust my heavenly Father to help me," he said.

When the camp ended, nobody wanted to go home. The seed of God's Word had been planted in the children's hearts and was already sprouting and growing. Later, when they attended their local churches, we heard that their young fervor sparked new life in their congregations.

Over the years since we began that camp ministry, I have continued to be awed at how God has used that camp. Today, many of the children who attended that camp serve God worldwide as pastors and teachers. Indeed the Yugoslavian pastors were correct in saying that many young women would follow me and enter the ministry. Even my four younger sisters did—and today, some of their children are leading camps!

That camp, for me, was like a little taste of heaven, a living symbol of Christ's love, His salvation, His mercy, and His grace. And through it, He planted a little bit of heaven in my heart so that I will never settle for less.

(This camp is still going on today. After our parents died, my sisters and I deeded the big house and land for a camp and conference center built on the property.)

Seeing children's lives changed through the camp increased my faith and vision. I knew God had put this burden on my heart. So, for the rest of the summer after that first children's camp was completed, I crisscrossed Yugoslavia, Hungary, and Romania, smuggling in children's materials and giving away Bibles.

At first, I traveled with a group of young Swedish people. The Swedish churches were very much involved in Eastern Europe, and I was happy they had invited me to help them as an interpreter. Since I knew the churches in my province, I could also act as a contact person. During those trips, I met people who were also interested in children's ministry.

After Yugoslavia, we went to Romania. Under President Ceausescu's dictatorship, the people had hardly any freedom, and the Christians suffered greatly under the strict laws.

In Romania, Bibles were so rare that it was common for a dozen believers to share one Bible. They would carefully write down the verses and memorize them in case someone would take their Holy Book away. Typically, if the communists found a Bible, they would confiscate it and most likely penalize the owner with a loss of privileges or general harassment. Even their children suffered consequences; sometimes, they were suspended from school or further study or sent to jail.

In Yugoslavia, it was not dangerous to own a personal Bible. Since we lived on a farm close to the borders, ministries from the West smuggled Bibles to our house all the time, and my mother hid them.

Accepting Bibles from the West was still illegal, but since my mother had become a Christian, she was willing to take the risk. Hundreds of Bibles and Christian books nestled under the mattresses in our home, waiting to be picked up and taken to Romania and other closed countries. Thankfully, we never got caught, but we had a few close calls.

These experiences of the past gave me courage for the present task. After several successful trips with the Swedish team, I traveled on by myself. I had done this before, but not as often.

My church would give me the address of a family—mostly Hungarians who lived in Romania—who would be receiving a Bible. I never knew where the addresses came from. That remained a secret. I would either memorize the address or write it on a tiny piece of paper. They instructed us, "If the police catch you, swallow the paper quickly so the receiving family will not be in trouble and end up in jail." Thankfully, I never had to do that.

Generally, I would travel during the daylight, hiding children's materials and some Bibles in my suitcase. Under the darkness of night, I would quietly navigate my way along pitch-black streets—there were no streetlights in many of the small villages—and walk along shadowy corridors to make my deliveries.

My senses were heightened in the darkness; every little noise rattled my nerves. I'd hear dogs barking and wonder if the police were nearby. Under the shroud of nightfall, it was quite an art to read the house numbers! Once I knew where the house was, I often circled the block to make sure no one was following me.

I don't think of my efforts as heroic, nor did I smuggle in a considerable quantity of Bibles. But the joyful responses of the people I met told me that my risk was well worth it.

One night I handed a Bible to a Hungarian family in Romania. They started to cry, smothering both the Bible and my face with kisses! The mother went on and on, looking into my eyes, and uttering her thanks over and over, *"Köszönöm, Köszönöm."* The sniffles and smiles and tears of these dear people stained my heart with awe and gratitude. I also had the privilege to bring them clothes, but that seemed minuscule compared to the gift of a Bible in their language.

More than once, I risked my life that summer.

Once, while sitting in my compartment on a train in Romania, I told my fellow travelers about Jesus. After a while, one person got up and left. When the train stopped at the next station, I felt a strong inner nudge to disembark. Though I sensed it was God's spirit warning me, my practical side argued, *But this is not my station!*

Nevertheless, the sense of danger became so strong, I finally obeyed. I slipped off the train and hid behind the train station's main building. When I peeked around the corner, I saw several police officers rush into the train, into the same car where I had been sitting. Now I knew that the person who had left the compartment so abruptly had reported me. I was so grateful that the Holy Spirit, once again, was taking care of me and that I had listened and obeyed.

The summer ended, and I returned to school in Germany without a penny in my pocket. I had spent all my money on the camp and in crisscrossing the European continent smuggling Bibles.

A few days after arriving at school, the president announced during our morning devotional time: "If you have not yet paid your tuition, please come to the office."

I walked to the office door, touched the doorknob, then turned and quickly headed down the hall toward the prayer room. "God, you know I'm penniless. Please provide for me," I prayed.

Throughout the week, I repeated that same routine every day. Whenever my hand touched the doorknob, I lost courage. So back to the prayer room I went.

What would happen when I told the secretary, "I don't have any money"?

Over the weekend, I ran into the secretary in, of all places, the school laundry room. "I wanted to talk to you all week," she said.

"Oh, really?" I asked as I tried to hide my anxiety by folding some clothes.

"Yes, but I was too busy," she continued. "I wanted to let you know that at the beginning of the week, somebody paid for your entire year of school."

My jaw dropped. "Who did this?"

"I cannot tell you," she replied. "The person wants to remain anonymous."

And nameless that person has remained until this book was published in German. After reading the book, my former roommate revealed that she had paid my school fees. It was a surprise to find this out forty years later. Not only that, but God saw fit to also provide me with shoes and clothing. For some reason, I had more money that year than any other year. I don't know where it all came from. All I can say is that our extremely generous Father cares well for His children. He knows what they need. I lacked nothing, not because of my striving, but because I let Him provide.

And He provided in a way bigger than my dreams.

COMFORTABLE SHOES AND A STOLEN HEART

*I felt like a tug-of-war was going on
between my head and my heart.*

My three new roommates—Sieglinde and two girls, both named Ingrid—and I spent much of the first week back at college that second-year filling our free afternoons with drinking coffee, sharing our stories, laughing, and crying together. It was a celebration of the amazing things God had done through us over the summer.

A summer of ministering in Eastern Europe had opened my eyes to the deep need there. Under the communist oppression, people were hungry and ripe for the gospel's freeing truths. I had seen the hand of God working in transforming lives. Now I was craving a future filled with ministry to the lost behind the Iron Curtain.

Furthermore, being the first woman from Eastern Europe at this college, I felt a profound responsibility. I wanted to focus all my attention on following Jesus. I was so committed that I was entirely blind to the many offers and advances coming my way from potential suitors. My heart was sold out to Jesus, and I did not want to be distracted.

Even so, I couldn't help but notice a dark, curly-haired Canadian with a deep, bass voice in the new freshman class. He wore a colorful green-checkered jacket, which among the grey and dark colors most of the German guys were wearing, made him stand out like a peacock among pigeons. He radiated self-confidence.

I found out his name was Ditmar. The rumor was that he had been a bank manager in British Columbia, Canada, before coming to this college in Germany. He came to "refresh his German."

Later on, I found out from a friend that the first day Ditmar saw me sitting across the cafeteria, he leaned over and asked, "Who is that cute chick over there?"

"Forget her!" his friend answered. "She is married to God! A lot of guys have tried to go out with her with no success."

"We'll see about that!" Ditmar replied and returned to eating his Wienerschnitzel and potatoes.

Although I was intrigued by this handsome Westerner, I had put a lock on my heart. *No, Elizabeth,* I told myself, *don't let go of your heart. Use your mind.* And my mind was telling me that no man from the West would ever want to move to the East where I wanted to live and work.

So I kept my heart locked tight for most of the year.

Then, one day toward the end of the year, our whole school went on an outing to Leer in Northern Germany. I was sitting next to one of my girlfriends on the bus. About halfway into the trip, Ditmar tapped my girlfriend on the shoulder.

"Would you trade seats with me?" he asked.

She looked at him, eyed me, then glanced at Ditmar's seat companion and said eagerly, "Yes." I peeked over my shoulder and saw that the man Ditmar had been sitting beside was another Canadian whom my friend liked.

I smiled at Ditmar as he settled into the seat beside me, but I cautioned my mind, *Guard your heart.*

I do not remember Ditmar's first words to me, but during the following hours, our conversation flowed—despite my stilted German—as if we had known each other for years. He asked me to tell him more about my life in Eastern Europe and my passion.

I began to lose control of my heart. *He may not be so bad,* I thought. I longed to know more about this mysterious Canadian.

Then Ditmar gently took my hand in his. "You have such beautiful hands."

I was hoping he wouldn't notice my blushing cheeks.

Oh no. I tried to stop the slow melt of my heart. *I cannot let myself be distracted.* I felt like a tug-of-war was going on between my head and my heart. I wasn't sure which would win out: reason or attraction.

That night, as I lay in my bed in the youth hostel, my heart won out. I couldn't "reason" myself to stop thinking of him, and I tossed and turned in a sleepless fit. It didn't matter how much I tried to keep myself from remembering him. My mind kept replaying our conversation.

Summer came, and we went our separate ways. I journeyed back to Yugoslavia to lead summer camps. At this time, several teenagers requested a camp for their age also. I organized it for them and invited Peter Kuzmic, my college friend, as the speaker. With his special message, he challenged the young people, many of whom heeded the ministry call. Several years later, he founded the respected Evangelical Theological Seminary in Croatia.

Ditmar stayed in Germany to help with camps there. Almost every day, though, I received a handwritten letter from him. His letters always made me feel special. He wrote to me about his activities. He also told me about his heart. He signed his letters with "xxx, Ditmar." I wasn't familiar with "xxx" and didn't know what it meant. Later, I blushed with embarrassment when someone told me it stood for "kisses."

Maybe once a week I wrote him back. Though I enjoyed receiving his letters, I kept thinking, *This won't work. We live in two different worlds. I want to work for God after graduation, and I don't know what Ditmar intends to do.*

Summer ended, and my final year of school commenced. Arriving the day before classes, I found myself standing in my room, looking out the window, hoping to see Ditmar. When he rounded the corner by the library, and his curly dark hair came into view, my heart skipped a beat. Later that evening, I saw him across the cafeteria, meeting up with his guy friends. The whole room was abuzz with the chatter and joy of reuniting friends—all of us telling each other our stories from a summer of work. But I had a hard time focusing my attention on anybody else.

Who was this stranger I had come to love? My mind asked my heart. I was surprised by how easily this question popped into my mind. I had never before admitted to loving him. I didn't want to love him.

Utterly uninterested in my dinner, I pushed my plate away. There was too much nervous activity going on in my stomach for me to eat.

A few days later, Ditmar asked me if I would meet him for coffee in the city. He wanted to meet me off campus, away from all the curious eyes. "And bring a photograph of yourself," he said. I thought this was strange, but I said I would.

Since it was a secret rendezvous, I took the train, and he came by car. We were to meet at the train station.

I arrived at the train station, but there was no sign of Ditmar.

Fifteen minutes passed, then thirty, then an hour, then an hour and a half—still no Ditmar. Two hours later, he finally arrived.

"Sorry I'm late," he said. "I had a flat tire and other car problems."

"That's okay," I said.

"You're still waiting," he said with a broad smile.

"Yes," I answered, but in my mind, I wondered, *What would make me wait two hours for this man?*

We left the train station and found a little place where we enjoyed coffee, cake, and conversation, even though my German was shaky. "Did you bring a photo?" he asked.

"Yes."

I took the photo out of my purse, showed it to him, and then put it back into my wallet. He looked disappointed, but I felt that I would commit myself to more than I was ready for by giving him the photo. Ditmar seemed to understand. "I don't want to push you if you're not ready yet," he said.

Later he told me he was thinking, *But a girl who waits for me for two hours—now that's the kind of woman I would like to have.*

In the end, we promised to pray about whether or not we should "officially" date. Ditmar also went to the school president and asked permission for us to meet once or twice a month.

"The president has agreed," Ditmar told me later that evening. "He congratulated me and said I'd picked a fine young woman."

I smiled.

We knew that dating was not encouraged at the college since we students were to keep our minds on our studies. Even so, they usually granted permission.

Now that we had permission, our next official date was in the kitchen of Emma Decker. She had been a missionary serving in China for many years until that country closed. Then she came to Germany to work. Her kitchen was tiny, with only a small table and two chairs. We sat across from each other, and as we were talking, I sensed the time had come for me to tell Ditmar about the ugly incident that happened to me just inside Austria seven years earlier. I did not want our relationship to grow any deeper without him knowing the truth of my past.

While I spoke, Ditmar's brown eyes filled with compassion. Somehow I managed to get through it, but then the dam broke, and my tears began to flow. Ditmar got out of his chair and gently pulled me into his arms. I could feel his strength seep into me.

"Elizabeth," he whispered, "I love you, no matter what happened back then. You are so special to me." He paused, then said, "Will you marry me?"

I couldn't believe what I had just heard. I had told this man the ugly, painful truth of my past, and he asked me to marry him. He loved me anyway!

I wanted to say "Yes," but instead, I said, "Let's pray some more about it."

God reminded me of His goodness as the words of the Bible kept running through my mind: "My beloved spoke and said to me, 'Arise, my darling, my beautiful one, come with me. See! The winter is past; the rains are over and gone. Flowers appear on the earth; the season of singing has come.'"[9]

WHITE SHOES IN THE SNOW

*His newfound passion for missions
wooed me even more.*

A few months later, Ditmar and I found ourselves once again separated
by several thousand miles. It was spring break, and the student body
split up to do ministry in many different countries. I went to Israel to
work on a kibbutz for a month. We picked grapefruit in the mornings
until 1:00 p.m., and in the afternoon, we were free to go sightseeing.
Ditmar chose to travel with a group to Romania.

The next time I saw Ditmar, I was surprised by the enthusiastic
report he gave of his trip. He kept talking about the country of Romania and its people with so much compassion. It had been a very
severe winter in Romania, he said, and the roads were an awful mess of
mud and potholes. Between the rains and the melting snow, tremendous flooding had occurred. Many people were displaced, losing their
homes, family treasures, and clothing. Furthermore, necessities such as
food and medicines were scarce.

Ditmar's team had taken half a dozen truckloads of food and
clothing to hand out to the people. Tucked inconspicuously between
the provisions and mountains of clothing were thousands of Bibles.
Their destination? The local churches would then distribute the goods
among the people who had lost not only their homes but hope as well.

"I want to go back there," Ditmar said excitedly. "The need is so
great." Then he laughed. "Just imagine—they gave me the head of a
chicken to eat." I smiled and explained that the chicken's head goes to
the guest of honor!

His adventures enthralled me. He told me how humbled he felt when he learned what Romanian believers sacrifice to live for Jesus. "People pay a high price to be a Christian in that country," he said. Still, they had such joy and courage in persecution and severe poverty.

"Their lives are simple," he said. "But they love receiving the Bibles even more than the food and clothing!" Romanian Christians expressed their gratitude to this group of ragtag college students who had sacrificed time and money to come to their country.

Ditmar's newfound passion for missions wooed me even more. At least now, I allowed myself to consider the possibility of sharing my life with him. Excitedly we talked about the mission, dreaming of what God might do in and through our lives.

It was time to have a conversation with my heavenly Father and ask myself a difficult question: *What's important to me about my future husband?*

I answered my question: *That he would love God with all his heart, strength, and mind and would love me and have a passion for missions.*

But what if he doesn't want to go to Eastern Europe? My heart still ached for the people there, and I knew God had planted in me a growing desire to minister to women and children. But did it have to be Eastern Europe?

As usual, when I was puzzled, I knelt beside my bed and said, "God, you are bigger than my dreams. You know. You see. You care. I trust You. But giving up this dream is not easy."

Then it hit me what I was saying. I was quiet for several minutes, then said aloud, "God, I want You to be my God, not my dreams. Do with them what you wish. I'm all yours."

In giving up my dream of pursuing missions in Eastern Europe, I felt the sting of death. It was all I'd thought of for so long. But I also felt an overwhelming peace in my decision to marry Ditmar.

When I said "yes" to Ditmar's proposal, the tug-of-war in my heart finally ended. We began to plan our wedding with great joy.

After graduation in May 1971, Ditmar traveled to my hometown and met my family. They would not be able to attend our wedding in

Ditmar's hometown of Vancouver, British Columbia. Only Charlotte, a friend from college, would be at the wedding as my maid-of-honor.

My family planned a large engagement celebration with about fifty people attending while Ditmar was there. It was a festive extravaganza complete with a sit-down dinner, dessert, and lots of joy. My friends were well pleased with my "catch." Mom and Dad loved Ditmar from the moment they met him. The way they fussed over him, I was almost jealous. *Hey, they love him more than me!* But I was also thrilled with their warm welcome of my future husband.

Shortly afterward, Ditmar flew to Vancouver, while I stayed another eight months in Yugoslavia. I had promised a Swedish Missions Organization supporting me to finish out the year and fulfill my commitment with them.

I spent those months organizing a children's camp and a youth camp in Subotica. It was beautiful to see young men and women dedicate their lives to God, then obey His calling to enter the ministry. Along with the camps, I continued working in my church and traveling to other cities. I also made a trip to Trieste, Italy, to buy beautiful white material, which I designed and sewed into a wedding dress for myself.

Even though my work with the ministry was exciting and fulfilling, I was eager to be with Ditmar. I had applied for my immigration papers, and the Canadian officials did a thorough check. I had to go through many tests and fill out many forms.

Still, the Canadian embassy officials were kind and gracious, unlike the ones at the Yugoslavian embassy. I was so emotionally exhausted, but my heart kept telling me, *Don't give up! Soon you'll be with Ditmar.*

Finally, at the beginning of December, I received the necessary papers for me to leave Yugoslavia. I packed my two suitcases with the wedding dress carefully tucked into one of them. My sister Rosie, her husband, and my mother accompanied me on the train as far as Belgrade. Then I caught an airplane on a transatlantic flight to North America. It all seemed so surreal.

Throughout the flight, I could barely eat or sleep. *Will Ditmar's family like me?* I kept wondering. *Will they accept me into their family?*

What a relief when I walked off the plane to see Ditmar waiting for me! He greeted me with a joyous embrace and a kiss on my cheek. Then he introduced me to his beaming family.

Peter, four years younger than Ditmar, gave me an exuberant hug. "You're exactly what the doctor ordered and what Ditmar has dreamed about since he was sixteen years old. God answered his prayers."

Everyone was so welcoming. Right away, I felt at ease with his two younger sisters, Betty and Evie. His mother even called me "daughter." But Ditmar's father was my favorite. He was everything I thought a father should be: kind, understanding, and protective.

On January 8, 1972, Ditmar and I were married. Standing at the altar of a church, before several hundred guests, we took our vows: "To have and to hold, for better or for worse, for richer or for poorer, in sickness and in health, till death do us part."

Long ago, I had concluded that I could never wear white on my wedding day because of my experience in Austria. After all, I had been stained, and white would be inappropriate. But during the last few years, God had brought much healing to my heart. I knew He didn't hold what had happened against me, and neither did Ditmar. To celebrate His full forgiveness, I had picked out that white fabric in Italy with great joy. And on my wedding day, I wore a white gown, white flowers in my hair, a long white veil, a white bouquet, and matching white shoes. Free and forgiven, I stood happily beside my groom.

Ditmar's grandfather, who was a pastor, conducted the wedding ceremony. For us, he had chosen the following Scripture passage where Ruth stated: "Don't urge me to leave you or to turn back from you. Where you go I will go, and where you stay I will stay. Your people will be my people and your God my God. Where you die I will die, and there I will be buried. May the Lord deal with me, be it ever so severely, if even death separates you and me."[10]

ELIZABETH MITTELSTAEDT

As he talked about Ruth's commitment to Naomi and the sacrifices she made, tears dampened my cheeks. God was writing a confirming exclamation mark on my heart.

Through the book of Ruth, God was also proclaiming to me that the "outsider"—the little village girl from communist Yugoslavia—would someday participate in a greater life-plan. It would be significant and redemptive not only in her life but in the lives of thousands of people and entire nations.

Yes, I promised both God and Ditmar as I spoke my "I do." *Lord, we will go together wherever You lead us.*

Almost as if on cue, millions of white snowflakes danced in the sky, dressing the city in white celebration. It was another unexpected exclamation point from God. I felt He was saying, "Elizabeth, my beloved, you are pure, white as snow, free to follow the dreams I've placed in your heart."

That day I delighted not only in Ditmar's love but also in God's love. For our wedding night, my husband had chosen a beautiful bridal suite in Vancouver. God crowned the night with wonder. The past was far behind me: I was made whole and free in the goodness of a loving Savior.

Grace. Marvelous, restoring grace.

FLIP-FLOPS IN THE SAND

All my life, I had dreamed
of going to America—until...

Wherever You lead, I will follow.

A year later, with two small suitcases in hand, Ditmar and I—now the proud owner of a Canadian passport—boarded a Greyhound bus that took us down the west coast of North America from Vancouver to Los Angeles. Ditmar was to finish his college degree at Vanguard University, and I would try to find work to help him through college. We couldn't believe we were headed to the land of sunshine and theme parks!

All my life, I had dreamed of going to America—the land of the free, the home of the brave. I envisioned a life of us taking long walks on endless beaches lined with palm trees and watching romantic sunsets together. America was the "good life"—a place where money grew on trees, and you could pursue your dreams. At least, others who had fled Yugoslavia and come to America had written home, filling our heads with a thirst for such freedom. Now it was my turn.

College started a week after our arrival. Immediately, the cost of living and the pace of life in California suffocated us. At first, we thought we would return to Vancouver to get the rest of our meager belongings, but we had already run out of money and time to do that. Quickly, we looked for an affordable apartment and jobs that would help us pay our expenses.

The only person we knew in California was B.T. Bard, a seventy-nine-year-old retired missionary from a German Lutheran family. He lived in a trailer park with Ada, his newlywed eighty-year-old bride. B.T. and Ada had known each other as missionaries in China. Both widowed, they had rekindled their friendship and were now "book-ending" their lives together. They helped us get plugged into a church right away.

We enjoyed B.T. and Ada's company very much, but their small trailer was too cramped for all four of us. Ditmar and I slept on the floor in their small guestroom. The house search was exasperating. For what we could afford, the pickings were slim. After one fruitless day, I returned home devastated.

Ada, made wise by her many years of life as a missionary, tried to comfort me: "God must have a better plan for you."

Ada was right. A week later, when she introduced us to a couple at church who owned several apartments, they offered us one.

"But how can we pay the rent?" I asked. "It is more than we can afford."

"No problem," the owners replied. "We'll let you live there in exchange for cleaning some of our rental houses."

We worked very hard, yet we still had little money—only what was left after I had worked hard all day or helped out at the church. I continued to sew all my clothes in my spare time. We fixed up our apartment so well that most people didn't notice how poor we were. Often we ate bread and jam for our meals.

"Lord, I'm so tired of bread and jam," I complained, but there was no answer.

Now I understood why the Israelites complained about eating manna every day in the desert. Why they had said, "If only we had stayed in Egypt." Like them, I wanted to whine for the if onlys—two of the saddest words in any language. But also, I remembered their wilderness wandering. What should have taken only eleven days stretched into forty years, not because of their enemy, but because they complained in their tents.

One thing was for sure: this Disneyland of sun and surf—the land we'd expected to be the promised land flowing with milk and honey—had deceived us. We were wandering in a desert.

It became the beginning of my "manna" time. God's provision from heaven would fall on time, every time. If I tried to grab for more than my daily share—wanting to build a sense of security—it rotted. Like when I took on one more job, which turned out to be more than my weakened body could handle. I'd come home totally exhausted, kick off my flip-flops, and with a sigh, plop myself down on the green sofa and cry.

But one fall day, as I came home from work, the Santa Ana winds were kicking up a dust storm. I hurried into my apartment just as millions of tiny grains of sand pelted the windowpane. I fell on my knees beside my bed and cried out: "God, how long do I have to do this hard work of cleaning houses? You know I want to work for you."

I swallowed little grains of sand in my mouth as I continued my complaint: "God, I feel like you've sent us into the wilderness and forgotten about us."

There was no reply. God's silence was deafening.

BABY SHOES AND DREAMS

*The joy of a little one growing inside me
overshadowed every other concern.*

The summer of 1974 was very hot. I felt nauseated and wondered if I was catching the flu. My body had been fragile ever since birth—diphtheria that my mother had suffered as she was pregnant with me had also weakened my health. I was continually susceptible to whatever colds and sicknesses were going around. Only this time, it felt different.

Then I realized my period was a few weeks overdue. *Oh, no! It is not the best time for a baby,* I thought.

"Honey, we're going to have a baby!" I exclaimed to Ditmar.

Ditmar's first reaction was like mine. "How will we make it? We can hardly feed ourselves, much less a child."

But soon, the joy of a little one growing inside me overshadowed every other concern. *Will it be a girl?* I wondered. *I would sew such beautiful dresses for her.* But then I'd think, *No, it's a boy.* I'm not sure what led me to that conclusion, but it felt right.

Then one day, two months into my pregnancy, I was too sick to go to work. I felt a jolt of pain in my side. "Can this be normal?" I wondered aloud.

I knew something was very wrong. The following day, a flow of blood showed me that I had lost my precious gift. My baby had died.

After I had run out of tears, I lay on the bed, motionless. I had no more words. I had no feeling. *He went to heaven so early,* I thought.

It took a while for me to sort out my turbulent emotions. How confusing it all was. First, a baby at an unexpected time. Then, our growing love for this child escalated each day. In preparation to welcome and nurture this little person, my body and emotions had crescendoed. Suddenly, he was gone. But my hormones raged on. Physically, mentally, emotionally, and spiritually, I hardly knew how to endure the abruptness of it all. *Miscarrying is like a sick prank,* I thought. *Your hopes are taken to the highest level, only to have them dashed at the lowest bottom.*

I kept asking God, "Why?" But I never received an explanation. Still, I sensed God was near me. Once again, I remembered His five words of promise: "I will never leave you."

For months, God listened to my honest ranting and questioning and never condemned me for the asking. He went with me on the roller coaster of my emotions. And I continued to invite Him to heal my broken heart.

I often dreamed of the little boy, or little girl—or both—that we would have down the road.

We went to see a doctor. After several tests, he called us into his office to share the results with us. He broke the news to us rather abruptly: "You will probably never have children."

We were so disappointed.

"Maybe you can adopt a child," the doctor said. "I know of a baby boy who will be up for adoption almost immediately."

Surprised but wondering if this was God's direction for us, we asked him to look into it.

A short while later, we got the news that the baby boy had died of heart failure soon after birth. Our hopes plummeted again. *So what else might God choose to do?* We hoped and prayed for a miracle.

But over the next twenty years, such a miracle didn't happen.

God made women with an innate drive to give life and to nurture it. I was no different. A strong desire would well up in me whenever I saw mothers with their little children—most especially at Christmas. As Miroslav Volf said in his book, *Free of Charge,* "I felt like a child in a large family, the only one to whom parents had forgotten a gift."[11]

"Next month, you will be pregnant," I tried to assure my empty heart and arms.

I kept waiting. Yet, I never got a positive result or an answer from God. Nothing broke our barrenness—not prayer nor fasting—but still, we hoped.

One day, while praying, I suddenly realized how I was letting my life pass me by. I was wasting energy by continuing to believe that only a child would solve this inner longing.

As I write these few paragraphs now about our twenty-year struggle with infertility, the words seem deficient.

A few years later, we tried to adopt another child. A missionary friend of ours told us about a young teenager who had gotten pregnant and wanted to abort the child.

"Would you be willing to adopt the baby?" she asked us.

"Yes," we said in unison. The thought of saving a baby's life gave us great joy. We tried to prepare our hearts for this new addition to our family. We looked forward to bringing our little bundle of joy home.

A few days before giving birth, the mother changed her mind and decided to keep the child.

More grief! More emptiness. More questions.

But we tried to hold on to our focus: *Lord, we still love You. Not our will, but Yours be done.*

Over time, when I saw my friends having children, I felt intense jealousy. It welled up in my heart whenever I was around other women with children.

One day, while reading a church newsletter, this poem hit home:

Envy stares at the other person, thinking:

I wish I had what you have!

Empathy looks at the other person, asking:

What do I have that I could give you?

Envy revolves around self and says, "Poor me!"

Empathy concentrates on others, saying, "Poor you!"

Envy destroys and paralyzes me.
Empathy revives and motivates me.

Envy is a deadly sin.
Empathy is a wonderful Christ-reflecting virtue.

The poem resounded deep in my heart, decrying the drastic difference between living and how I wanted to live. I copied the poem into my journal so I could say it each time my heart was tempted to envy.

In time, God freed me from envy and gave me empathy. I learned to define my life by what I had—and to rejoice in it. Little by little, He gave me the grace to accept that I would never experience the gift of motherhood.

Little did I know that one day, God would even use this experience for His more significant cause.

SUNDAY SHOES AND AN OPEN DOOR

As my English improved,
a new world opened up to me.

Ditmar and I continued to work, and he continued to study. He had finished his undergraduate degree in theology and was now pursuing his M.Div at Biola University in LaMirada, California, in the Los Angeles basin. At that time, our church hired Ditmar as a part-time pastor. He worked in the church with children, a perfect outlet for us. How we enjoyed pouring our love into these children! Such work helped to ease the heartache for our own little ones.

I also found a part-time job with Wycliffe Bible Translators. Our new jobs brought us great joy. Moreover, the hours were not as long or hard, and I finally had time to sew lovely, new dresses again, not just for myself but also for my sisters back in Yugoslavia. I was able to find beautiful material for a dollar a yard. Then I sewed my version of the simple but elegant cuts I found in *Vogue* magazine. When my sisters in Yugoslavia received the dresses, they would write and tell me they felt like princesses.

As my English improved, a new world opened up to me. I discovered Christian books and magazines and felt like a little girl in a candy store. I remember reading Catherine Marshall's book *Christy*, and although I understood only half of what I was reading, I knew this was "my" kind of world. Eagerly I applied myself to learn the language faster, so I could read more about God's stories.

Other things that helped us during those desert years in California were our friendships. B.T. and Ada were especially supportive. They took us under their wings, and we spent many happy hours sitting around our kitchen table, laughing and discussing life. They encouraged and challenged us. No question was too stupid to ask, and many times, their simple wisdom would gently correct us far better than any long lecture would have done. They were always so generous and compassionate and had a real heart for people who didn't know Jesus Christ. They were amazing models to us of faith, hospitality, and generosity.

We had many guests come to "the little yellow house" during our years in California. Our international guests always wanted to see the Pacific Ocean and Disneyland. I was excited to take our guests to these places. My favorite ride was "It's a Small World After All"—the song would ring in my ears for hours. Disneyland helped refresh my soul with a lot of laughter and childlike joy, and the vastness of the ocean often brought perspective. It was nice to see both our laughter and mood increase after those devastating first two years. One friend said, "Our lack of laughter seems in proportion to our lack of faith." Yes, God's joy was prevailing and, perhaps our faith was growing too.

We were not camping in the desert anymore. California felt like home now as we engaged with people and built relationships. God taught us, whether we lived in Vancouver or Santa Ana, to make the best of it. Now we were not just surviving; we were thriving and loving it. Only from time to time was I sad, thinking of the child we'd lost. Then tears would inadvertently fill my eyes.

With some guest speakers from foreign countries coming through and sharing awesome stories of God's provision, power, and compassion, our hearts returned to the dream of serving overseas. During one lunch, a guest speaker asked, "What do you two dream of doing after Ditmar finishes graduate school?"

With one voice, we responded: "Missions!"

"Really?" he said. "If you're serious about missions, it would be better for you to move to Illinois. California is too crowded with missionaries and pastors."

Illinois? I thought. *We don't know anybody there.*

Within minutes, our guest called his friend in Chicago, Bill Bell, who pastored Calvary Temple. It just so happened that he was looking for an assistant pastor responsible for Christian education.

"Bill, you have to meet this young couple," we overheard him saying on the phone. "You will like them."

The following month we found ourselves on an airplane to Chicago. We sat quietly beside each other. So many questions went through my head: *What will our future be? Will they take us? Is this God's will?*

As the plane coasted into O'Hare International Airport, we looked out the window and marveled at the immensity of the city spread out underneath us.

"Honey, it's so flat," I said. "There are no mountains and no ocean!" I took a deep breath, then continued, "I heard it's freezing in the winter." Looking at Ditmar's face, I could tell that he had his apprehensions. Already, we felt homesick for California.

In the evening, we met the church board at the pastor's house. As we enjoyed homemade ice cream, we cautiously looked about us. We knew these people had come to "check us out," and they were not at all subtle about it. They bombarded us with questions. Ditmar and I must have looked nervous, for, all of a sudden, Rob Brendel, who also had a German background, said, "Well, it's nice to get to know some other displaced persons." That made us laugh and put us more at ease.

After the long evening of meeting new people and answering a barrage of questions, Ditmar and I were exhausted. We retired to Pastor Bell's guestroom just as a vast thunderstorm shook the city. We had never experienced anything like it. Lightning flashed across the sky, followed by loud claps of thunder. But we were so tired that we fell asleep anyway. About midnight, there was another explosion of thunder. A bright lightning flash followed by a loud crash.

Ditmar grabbed me tightly. "Honey!" he screamed. "Jesus is coming back!"

After that, sleep was gone.

During breakfast, everyone at the table was quiet. No one asked the traditional American question, "How'd ya sleep?" No one else seemed to have been bothered by the terrible thunderstorm.

Are these storms typical? I wondered.

Suddenly, Pastor Bell burst out laughing, and everyone joined in. We wondered what was so funny. Among fits of laughter, he said that he'd heard Ditmar screaming last night that Jesus was coming back! I started laughing, too, remembering how tightly Ditmar had held on to me.

This "night-scream" has become one of our running jokes throughout the years. Sometimes when people tease Ditmar, "Why did you hold on to Elizabeth so tightly?" he answers, "My only thought was: If she goes to heaven, I'm going too."

That Sunday night, they asked Ditmar to deliver a sermon. Again, we knew this was a "test" of sorts: if the congregation liked it, they would vote us in. I sat in the front pew, praying for him. Though I felt the pressure, I comforted myself that if things did not work out, we could always go back to California, and that wouldn't be so bad.

That evening we received a 100 percent "yes" vote to bring us on staff. Later the pastor's wife said to me, "While Ditmar was preaching, we were also watching you. How a wife reacts to the husband's sermon says almost as much as the sermon itself."

Whew, I'm so glad I didn't fail us there! I thought.

We told Pastor Bell that we would have an answer for him within one week. We wanted to pray and think it through some more and get some wise counsel.

On Monday, we returned to Los Angeles. As we neared the city, we both felt in our hearts that it was time to move on. Although many details remained a mystery to us, we knew it was time to take another step of faith.

The following weeks we packed up our belongings. As I held my flip-flops, I thought back on the difficulties of our first two desert years here. I was glad they were now but a memory and grateful that God had not remained silent. Yes, the first two years had been painful but purposeful. Then two beautiful years had followed. While visiting Palm Springs, California, I had seen the beautiful cactuses that bloomed in the desert. *Just like our lives,* I thought. *Like a prickly cactus, we, too, can bloom in the desert.*

Yes, during the last four years, God had pushed us out of our comfort zone. In the desert, God was teaching us not to rely on our sufficiency but His. Here we had developed an appetite for manna, which only God can provide. He weaned us off the breast milk of people-dependency. He had chosen a new way of guiding and providing. Often the path led through unfamiliar territory and anxiety. But He was writing our destiny. He knew the way, yet it was up to us to follow in obedience. This desert experience had been a growing-up time for us.

We said our good-byes, loaded our things into a U-Haul truck, and pulled away from our dear little yellow house that held so many precious memories. During those "manna years," God had allowed us to experience hunger, brief homelessness, loneliness, and loss. And He had built empathy in us toward other people experiencing the same. Little did I realize then that this was a preparation for another future assignment.

Before starting up the car, Ditmar and I prayed a very long "Thank you." Then we began the long drive to the city of Chicago.

HIGH HEELS IN CHICAGO

We certainly didn't feel like praying together,
but it was the one thing, perhaps, that saved our marriage.

Five years earlier, Ditmar and I had promised the Lord and each other, "Wherever You lead us, we will follow," and now we found ourselves living in Chicago, Illinois. Besides its notorious windy weather, we found out a few of Chicago's other reputations. In the 1930s, it was a city of "gangsters" with Al Capone "ruling" (some would say "tormenting") the metropolis. Half a century before Capone, there was a tremendous spiritual revival under the evangelist D.L. Moody. And everywhere we went, we read, on T-shirts and other touristy trinkets, the phrase that renowned crooner Frank Sinatra had made famous: "Chicago Is My Kind of Town." We wondered how Chicago would fit us. What kind of city would it be for us?

Ditmar went to work right away at the church, and I found a part-time job designing clothes. I had to wear a lot of high heels; the higher, the better. As I packed away my flip-flops, I chuckled to myself. "Lord, this is a far cry from cleaning rooms in California."

The first month in town, we stayed in Pastor Bell's guest room. Once again, we were on the hunt for our own place to live and finding it difficult to locate anything suitable. One day, Pastor Bell suggested, "Why don't you buy a house?"

Ditmar and I listened politely, but I kept thinking, *There's no way we can afford a house.* My husband must have felt the same thing, for he explained to Pastor Bell that our entire savings were comprised of one hundred dollars. But the pastor was intent on helping us. Through some friends, he arranged for the financing so we could get a mortgage. Ditmar's parents loaned us the down payment. Within a few weeks, we had purchased our own home in an Italian neighborhood. We were so excited!

We enjoyed working at the new church. With a smaller congregation—three hundred compared to one thousand—we found it easier to connect with people. The other three pastors and their wives also became dear friends. Pastor Bell's wife, Joan, was a tremendous support to me. She had a great passion for teaching the Word of God to others.

Though we did miss the mountains and ocean in California, it took us no time at all to fall in love with the Midwest. Besides working at the church, Ditmar attended Northern Baptist Seminary to finish his Master's degree. We talked less and less about Santa Ana—only when the winter hit and the whole city of Chicago lay buried in snow, and we shivered in the icy winds.

During our second year, Ditmar and I were caught up in the whirlwind of ministry. Although we enjoyed it immensely, we were finding less and less time together as a couple.

One evening as we were leaving for church, I didn't see a frozen puddle in our backyard. I stepped on it and slipped, crashing to the ground. As my head hit the frozen ground, it felt as if an iron fist had punched it hard. The doctor diagnosed a concussion, and for the next few weeks, I had to stay in bed.

Suddenly, everything stopped. My ministry teaching children. My part-time job as a fashion designer. There was an irony about that, for my red Christmas dress design had just won the first-place prize in the contest of "simple, elegant design." Now here I was, confined to bed. I could no longer send home beautiful dresses for my younger sisters, which had boosted their self-esteem and been such a great financial help to my mother. All of this was gone.

I had plenty of time to reflect on these changes.

I realized that I'd been so busy working for Jesus that I had little time for Him.

"I'm so sorry, God," I said. "I don't want to miss You while ministering in Your name." Yes, I was guilty: I'd been carried away in the whirlwind of big city life and the many ministry opportunities and had neglected my quiet time with God and even with Ditmar.

During this time, Ditmar and I did a lot of heart-searching as a couple. Lately, never-ending demands of ministry and life had consumed us so much that we hadn't had time for each other. No more time for talks, tenderness, and quiet, precious moments. We'd become irritable and argumentative. Ditmar would come home late from work. We'd eat our supper in silence, then get ready to be back at church by 7:00 p.m. Or Ditmar would hide in his office to study while I focused on sewing. In time, we grew apart to the point where we were afraid to talk to each other, lest we'd argue.

Still, we clung to our habit of praying together before going to sleep. Every evening, we would kneel beside the bed, each on our side, and commit ourselves to God.

One night Ditmar prayed, "We are hurting, God. We long for the fresh wind of Your love."

Now, as I was lying in bed, week after week, I had a lot of time to reflect and pray on my relationship with Ditmar. I also prayed for change. But it wouldn't be easy. We had some vicious arguments and hurt each other deeply. Sometimes I felt like I couldn't go on. I felt so alone with my problems. I had no relatives in Chicago who could encourage me, and I couldn't share my burdens with friends from church because Ditmar was one of the pastors. Sometimes my problems seemed insurmountable. But divorce was out of the question for both of us. During times of deep discouragement, I'd hear the enemy whisper, "You are not good enough for Ditmar. He would be better off without you."

And still, we maintained our habit of praying together in the evening. One night, as we knelt beside our bed, both of us started to sob. We were tired of the distance and heartache. Finally, we let go of our stubborn pride and asked each other for forgiveness. In that moment, a dark veil was lifted from us. We got up from our knees and ran toward each other. As Ditmar held me, I kept saying, "It's my fault; please forgive me."

"No, honey," Ditmar said, "it's my fault; please forgive me."

We kept on asking each other for forgiveness, not even sure what for. But the cloud of oppression had lifted. (Ditmar and I have often talked about this time, trying to pinpoint the problem so that in the future, we'll be able to avoid it from happening again. But we could never really put our finger on the source of our trouble. Sure, there were obvious reasons, such as not spending enough time with each other or ignoring each other because we were too busy to have the energy to work through our annoyances. But the problem had become so severe that we both despaired of living. The only thing that makes sense to us now is that, during this time, we were undergoing demonic oppression. Once it was broken, our fellowship was restored.)

Throughout the night, we held each other. Pain surrendered to peace. The walls that had separated us for half a year came tumbling down by honest talk and mutual surrender. Something (Someone) broke the rising darkness around us, and God set us on a new path toward greater intimacy and freedom in our marriage.

During that dark time, I don't know what made us hold onto our prayer habit. We certainly didn't feel like praying together, but it was the one thing, perhaps, that saved our marriage. Now we recommitted ourselves to stay sensitive toward each other and God. The wounds we had inflicted on each other didn't heal overnight, of course. Still, we began guarding our time together, watching our words, speaking openly and honestly about our feelings, and telling each other our likes and dislikes. And we determined to trust God to carry us through any future trying times. We would never again underestimate the power of prayer.

King Solomon wrote, "Enthusiasm without knowledge is no good; haste makes mistakes."[12] Best-selling author John Ortberg said, in his book *The Life You Always Wanted*: "When I first moved to Chicago, I called a friend—the wisest spiritual man I know—and asked him, 'What do I need to do to be healthy spiritually?' He said, 'You must ruthlessly eliminate hurry from your life.' There was a long pause, and

I finally said, 'Okay, I wrote that one down. Now, what else do you have to tell me, because I don't have much time, and I want to get a lot of wisdom out of this conversation.' He replied, 'There is nothing else.' As hard as it was to realize for me, hurry is an inward condition whereby I want to cover up the emptiness of my heart."[13]

I had been so preoccupied with ministry that I hadn't stopped to receive love from my heavenly Father. I had been running on empty myself for far too long. Consequently, I hadn't been able to give love to my husband, who was more precious to me than anything or anyone else in the world. I couldn't blame anyone but myself. I needed to change my thinking about what really matters in life. I determined that, in the future, the filling of my soul had to be top priority.

Both Ditmar and I discovered how much we had longed for closeness and intimacy—while we kept ourselves apart from each other. We wanted that deeper relationship—not just for our individual well-being but also for the other person.

That day we took out our wedding album and reminded ourselves and each other of our commitment. That beautiful white January day in Vancouver was only the beginning of walking the same path together. It was so good to know that God was on the journey with us through sweet and bittersweet times.

MOVING SHOES AND
A CHRISTMAS TO REMEMBER

God was preparing us for another move.
All that remained now was to wait
and see what He would do next.

The third year in the Windy City, God whispered to both of our hearts: "Prepare for change."

"What?" I asked the Lord. "Didn't we just move from California? I don't think I'm ready for more change."

Although both of us sensed the Lord's whisper of a new direction, we were completely unsure what His words meant.

Then the call came. As Ditmar was finishing up his Master's degree, he got an offer from a respectable church in Chicago to be their senior pastor. They said he would be free to work on his doctorate as well. It seemed like a dream come true! We liked Chicago and, during the past years, had become comfortable here. We had a house and good friends. Our renewed love for each other had increased our desire to serve God. We liked living in this city so much that we'd adopted Frank Sinatra's slogan: "Chicago is my kind of town"!

But one afternoon, as I was opening the door to the backyard, the wind seemed to carry a strong message: "Hold all of this very loosely. You will move to another country."

"God, is that You? Did I hear that correctly?" I knew it was God's message for me, but I kept the words hidden in my heart. I waited before telling my husband.

A few days later, Ditmar and I enjoyed one of his favorite meals: German rouladen with spaetzle. During dinner, he said, "Honey, I called a sending agency today and asked them some questions about foreign service. I wanted to know if they are sending missionaries to Eastern Europe. But they aren't. It's too dangerous, they said, and those who used to work there have moved to the West." I must have looked surprised, for Ditmar quickly added, "Don't worry, honey. I was just curious to see if God may still have foreign service in mind for us."

"You don't need to apologize," I said with a big smile.

Then I told him about the strong impression I'd received a few days earlier. We were excited to realize that God had given each of us a definite call. God was preparing us for another move. All that remained now was to wait and see what He would do next.

In the following months, we gathered information about various mission opportunities. During one interview with the Assemblies of God missions board, Dr. Hogan, the director, asked us, "Where would you like to go?"

Ditmar replied. "We are willing to go wherever you think we would fit best."

In our hearts, though, we were thinking of Eastern Europe. We had often talked about our past experiences of ministry there. But we also knew that the board was not sending missionaries into communist countries at the time.

"What about Germany?" Dr. Hogan continued. "We've just opened a college there for Distance Education (ICI University), and we need a director. Since you both speak German, you would fit perfectly. From there, you could travel to Eastern Europe."

Ditmar was overcome with emotion. He explained to the board, "When I was traveling throughout Germany, in the back of my mind, I kept thinking, *I will come back here someday.*"

He explained that his grandfather had been held in a Russian concentration camp (Gulag) for five years near the Russian Ural Mountains during World War II. "It was a miracle he survived," he said. "When Grandfather got out of the camp, he went to Bremen, in northern Germany. After I was born, my family (including Grandpa) immigrated to Canada. My parents never revisited Europe, and they discouraged us from going there."

Sure enough, when we told Ditmar's family that we had accepted an assignment in Germany, his mother was devastated. "Why do you have to go so far away?" she said. "America and Canada need pastors, too. Can't you just stay in North America?"

Uncle Kurt, on the other hand, was more encouraging. "Your grandfather left Germany, but Germany never left him," he said. "He prayed daily for Germany and the Eastern European countries. Little did he know that his grandson would be an answer to his prayers!" He smiled as he added, "Now the third generation will follow in his footsteps. How proud your grandfather would be to know you are going back to Europe to minister in Christ's name."

Maybe Grandfather did know, I thought. He had chosen to preach about Ruth at our wedding ceremony. And like her, we had made a promise: "Wherever you send us, we will go." Back then, we had no idea that Grandfather had prayed for Germany—both the East and the West—for many years.

Ditmar and I sat in wonder. *With God, nothing is random,* I thought. *And He makes no mistakes.* From flip-flops to high heels and now to German clogs, every step had been prepared for us. Now, this thread of Ruth's words to Naomi kept mysteriously showing up as a reminder to us of God's providence and kindness.

As we attended the School of Missions, I learned much about nations and cultures. I especially liked the class on anthropology and Joyce Booze's class on how to write a newsletter. For some reason, she invited me into her office to help write my story. Again, I saw myself as a child, writing with a pencil's stub or scratching in the dust. She didn't know, of course, how she was rekindling my childhood dream.

Once again, we found ourselves saying good-bye to good friends and mentors. Max Lucado, pastor, and best-selling author, once said that the missionary trail is stained with farewell hugs and good-bye tears. We were beginning to understand this more clearly. We felt the "bittersweetness" of it all keenly—grieving the loss of friendships, but at the same time, being very excited about all that God had ahead.

During the next few months, we traveled to many different churches. We talked to hundreds of individuals to raise the financial and prayer support we needed to work with the International Correspondence Institute (ICI). Choosing to depend upon another person's generosity is both humbling and amazing. Along with saying good-bye to people, we also had to say good-bye to belongings: things we couldn't take with us. I found some golden brown aluminum pots and told myself, "I've never really liked these." I took them off the shelf and put them into a bag to give to a friend. But as she walked away with the pots, I was overcome with tears.

Confused, I went back into the kitchen and, looking around, began to realize how much my heart was attached to old, familiar things—like aluminum pots.

Pull yourself together! I told myself. *God has been calling you to serve Him for a long time already. And now that He is leading you and your husband into a broader ministry, you should be happy, not sad.*

Still, I could not deny that fear had a grip on my heart. Being a faith-supported missionary did not promise a firm, secure income. Financially, we'd be dependent on God and the charity of others.

I stared at the empty shelves and wondered, *What does the future hold?*

The holidays were fast approaching. I enjoyed Christmas in Chicago, with the festive store windows, wreaths and twinkling lights, the parties, and musical cantatas. And the presents—so many of them!

All of this was such a stark contrast to the Christmases I knew growing up in communist Yugoslavia. On Christmas Eve, we'd sit around the old farmhouse as Grandpa read the Christmas story. As a present, I received a large, shiny orange—as I did every year. Christmas wasn't a comfortable and accepted holiday in my communist homeland. The communists had tried hard to eradicate it. My family could only celebrate Christmas in the evening if it were on a weekday because otherwise, we had to be in school. Those who were absent were dutifully "noted" as being suspect of celebrating a Christian holiday. The teachers interpreted the absence as a protest against communism. Some teachers even dropped the missing students' grades so drastically that they could not advance to the next grade.

I had grown so fond of the new Christmas traditions we'd begun in America. Realizing that this Christmas would be our last in Chicago, I wanted to make it extra special. I started decorating, baking, and planning parties with friends. On a piece of paper, I wrote my wish list: a flannel nightgown, a bottle of perfume, and a pair of brown gloves to match the cape I had sewn.

But a few days later, before I could divulge my wish list, Ditmar looked at me across the breakfast table and said, "Honey, you know we'll have a major cut in our income going into missions. Let's start now to prepare for the changes. This Christmas, let's settle for just one present."

With that, he left for the office.

My heart sank. Sadness swept over me as I remembered my childhood Christmas in Yugoslavia with only an orange for a present. *Will I be able to give up all the things that make Christmas so special to me?*

We had a few friends over for a quiet Christmas Eve celebration, and when the last couple left, Ditmar said, "Okay, honey, let's open our gifts."

Sure, one present. I thought—*big deal.*

Ditmar handed me a beautifully wrapped box. Inside was a lovely ivory sweater. I was touched and thanked him for his thoughtfulness. Then he gave me four more packages.

I was stunned, then upset. "I thought we had agreed on only one!"

"These aren't from me," he said. "They're from some friends at church."

I started with the biggest box. Carefully I removed the large bow and shiny paper. The present was from a boutique, and as I pulled back the tissue around the gift, I discovered a long-sleeved nightgown decorated with lace. It was stunning.

The next little package was decorated with yellow paper and tied with a fancy ribbon. When I ripped it open, it was my favorite perfume.

The third was a long, thin box from my favorite department store. Inside were soft brown leather gloves, a perfect match for the cape I'd just finished sewing.

I remembered my wish list: a flannel nightgown, a bottle of perfume, and a pair of brown gloves to match my cape.

There was no way the women had known about my list. Not even Ditmar knew it.

I picked up my fourth package. *What could be in it?* I wondered. When I lifted the lid, I saw an elegant silver dinner bell. *What do I need a dinner bell for?* I thought. I'll be glad if I have enough food for Ditmar and me.

Holding the shiny bell in my hand, I saw my reflection very clearly. Suddenly, a Bible verse came to mind: "For you know that it was not with perishable things such as silver or gold that you were redeemed from the empty way of life handed down to you from your ancestors, but with the precious blood of Christ, a lamb without blemish or defect."[14]

Just then, a gentle whisper came to my heart: "Elizabeth, you are more valuable to me than silver and gold. You don't need to be afraid. Wherever you go, I will take care of you. And I know your every need. Haven't I proven it by granting you every item on your wish list?"

I felt so loved and cherished.

Once, when I was speaking in a big church, I wanted to explain how much God loves me. English was relatively new to me. As I was groping for words, I exclaimed, "I don't know why God is so crazy about me." My audience roared with laughter at this. I didn't know I'd used a familiar colloquialism. Since then, my friends tease me about this remark.

But it's true. God is crazy about you and me.

That Christmas, there was more—abundantly more. A few days later, Ditmar took me to the jewelers. "I ordered something for you," he said with a delightful smile.

Then he displayed a beautiful wedding set with a diamond. "I should have given this to you for our engagement and on our wedding day," Ditmar explained. "But as you know, we were too poor then. Over the last ten years of our marriage, I have been collecting my pennies, and now is the best time to give you the ring."

I was speechless. Overwhelmed. Amazed. Yes, throughout the years, I had admired other women's diamond wedding sets. All I had was a simple gold wedding band. Sometimes I'd hide my hand because I didn't want people to notice it. God had heard even that desire of my heart. Ditmar and I agreed that I should wear my new ring the day we began our new journey. We waited until we got comfortably seated on the airplane. Then, as Ditmar looked deep into my eyes, he slid the ring onto my finger. That certainly made the plane ride more romantic!

I couldn't get over the "simple" Christmas Day, which turned out to be the most extravagant. As I leaned back in my airplane seat, I kept looking at my diamond ring, reflecting the light in rainbow colors. I kept recounting God's generosity to me over the past months. The seven colors of the rainbow reminded me of our covenant to each other and to God. I heard His gentle assurance again: "Elizabeth, do you remember the time when you sat on that wooden bench listening to Olga Olsson? Do you remember what you told me: 'God, in case you ever need another woman, I surely would love to work for you!'? Well, now is your time."

IN MY FATHER'S SHOES

I had longed for my father's approval so much!
If only he had said, even just once, "I love you..."

It felt wonderful to be back in Germany, the country where Ditmar and I met and fell in love. We were excited to reconnect with some dear friends, such as the Williscrofts, Olga Olsson, and Emma Decker, and continue to learn from their great wisdom and love. They had become like family to us, and we celebrated holidays, such as Thanksgiving and Christmas, together. As I watched them, their love touched me. They became my role models. I wanted to pattern my life after theirs. These friends demonstrated what a loving family should be like by their respect for each other—their support and encouragement. They loved God, loved others, and helped people find God. I, too, longed to leave impressions on others. I didn't want to pass through this life without a passionate purpose.

As our airplane flew over Frankfurt, I remember looking out the window and seeing below us a field of cabbages in perfect rows. During the first few months of setting up house, I discovered that everything in Germany was as orderly and clean as those cabbage rows.

We quickly found a place to live, and, yes, we renovated this house also. When people leave a rental unit in Germany, it's not uncommon for them to take nearly everything with them, including the carpet, kitchen cabinets, and lights. Thankfully, the previous renters had left the bathtub, some sinks, and the toilet! A few light bulbs dangled from the ceiling. We felt like we were moving into an old warehouse. Considering how very precise and methodical the Germans typically are, this perplexed me.

I considered myself a tidy housekeeper, but when I looked out my kitchen window, I saw my neighbor lady mopping the steps outside her house every morning! I could not warm up to the idea of scrubbing my outdoor steps every day.

Living in Europe again, I was closer to my family; at least no ocean separated us. Sometimes my sisters came to visit us in Germany and always returned home with their suitcases full of beautiful clothes I had made for them. When my sister Maria announced she was getting married, I altered my wedding dress so she could wear it. She looked so beautiful in it. In the following years, my wedding dress continued to travel to Eastern European countries, and many young women used it for their weddings. Moreover, Ditmar and I made several trips ourselves to Eastern Europe to help with camps or visit different churches. It was always the highlight of the year for us.

A year later, on a cold fall day, my sister Rosie phoned to tell me that Dad was in the hospital and very sick. I made plans to visit him, but she called that he was gone the very next morning.

So instead of going to Yugoslavia to see my father, I went there for his funeral. Yes, it was painful to lose my father. But I grieved more for myself. I had longed for my father's approval so much! If only he had said, even just once, "I love you." But he never did.

As the funeral went on, the pastor reflected how Dad must be enjoying heaven. The pastor had served Dad communion after his confession. He said Dad had shared how sorry he was for the pain and suffering he had caused the family because of his drinking. The pastor talked about how beautiful grace is and that God forgives all our sins if we ask Him.

At that moment, I was shocked by the intensity of my thoughts. *God, this isn't fair.*

God reminded me, "Did I make you pay for your sin?"

I hung my head, embarrassed. "No, Jesus paid it all on the cross." Also, I remembered how generous my heavenly Father was to me as I returned to Him. He had waited for me, just as He had waited for my father.

But I couldn't help my feelings. I felt cheated as I watched the coffin lowered into the grave. They forever buried my chance for his approval and love under a pile of dirt.

As I was trying to comfort my sister Edit, who was weeping bitterly, she pulled away from me. "You don't understand what it means to lose a father!" she said angrily.

What does that mean? I wondered, confused. *He's my father, too.* But it was not the time to ask any questions.

During my remaining days in Yugoslavia, the extended family reflected on Father's childhood. I learned that he, too, had tasted pain in his youth. After the communists took over Yugoslavia, we lost many of our possessions. Like so many men in our village, my father was so bitterly disappointed that he turned to alcohol. Later, after he became a Christian, he quit drinking for several years. But, sad to say, old patterns die hard. As life continued to disappoint him, my dad fell back into drinking. Soon he used the little money we had to buy booze while we went without necessities. When he was drunk, occasionally, he became verbally abusive. He used alcohol to ease the pain of his disappointment in life. He'd never moved on from that disappointment until the last couple of days before he died. And I'd missed that one, the brief possibility of connection.

I returned to Germany, grieving and disappointed. After I'd aired my thoughts and feelings to Ditmar, I prayed: "Lord, forgive me for holding on to unforgiveness unconsciously against my father for so long. Thank You for showing me." Then I wrote in my journal: Dad, I respect you for raising me, and I forgive you for not giving me the love I so deeply craved. Lord God, please help me let that disappointment go.

Similar issues drew young women to me. Our home was always open to those who needed to talk. One evening, over coffee and cookies, a young woman shared with me the pain from her past. I encouraged her, but mostly I just listened. As she talked, she realized, for the first time, having a choice to make: moving through her bitterness into hope or staying mired in that bitterness. When she left our home that day, she'd made her decision. Her face radiated with joy and hope for the future.

Amazed at the Spirit's work, I knelt beside my chair. "Lord, I want to know You more," I said. "I want to be a channel of hope to others. Please use me to encourage others like this woman tonight. Drive my bitterness far from me. Thank You for loving me just as I am, but also for helping me become the person You've called me to be. I want to be passionately committed to the purpose You have for my life."

Little did I know that being a channel of God's healing would mean experiencing more brokenness.

LOW HEELS IN THE VALLEY OF PAIN

*It was maddening for Ditmar, who likes to fix things,
to stand by helplessly while I suffered.*

I was missing two teeth, so in 1984 I went to see a dentist somebody had recommended to me. When I arrived at his office, I was surprised to see an older man. It seemed to me, from his actions, that he should probably retire soon.

What I thought would be "routine" turned out to be a torment. One hour passed, then two. I could no longer hold my mouth open, so the dentist's wife, who was his assistant, forced my mouth open for another three hours. The dentist was grinding off three teeth to prepare for a bridge, but the pain in my jaw traveled throughout my whole body.

When the dentist finished five hours later, I could hardly talk or swallow. "It is so painful," I barely mumbled to the doctor.

"You'll get over it," he said and dismissed me promptly from his office.

At the time, I didn't realize that dentist had done irreparable damage. But during the following months, the pain grew even worse and began to affect my ability to concentrate and even continue with regular daily activities.

We asked the church to pray for me, thinking of the Scripture: "Is anyone among you sick? Let them call the elders of the church to pray over them and anoint them with oil in the name of the Lord. And the prayer offered in faith will make the sick person well; the Lord will raise them up. If they have sinned, they will be forgiven."[15]

Six months later, we sought the help of a jaw specialist. After he'd examined me, he shook his head. Turning to his colleague, he said quietly, "What a butcher job! Shame on our profession."

"No more high heels for you," one doctor told me. "This is bad for your posture and affects the pain in your neck."

We continued to seek help from different specialists, but several caused further damage by performing unnecessary root canals and tooth extractions instead of helping.

I often poured out my frustration to God either out loud or in shaky writing in my journal. I filled page after page with my complaints, and when my journal was full, I burned it. Hearing me bad-mouthing God wouldn't do me or anybody else any good. But I was learning to be honest with God as I knew He wanted me to be.

One morning, while reading my Bible, I came upon the verse, "But I will restore you to health and heal your wounds."[16]

What a promise! It was a tiny seed that gave me hope for the future.

After the odyssey from dentist to dentist in Germany, we returned to the U.S. for treatment.

The following year, I checked into the Mayo Clinic in Rochester, Minnesota, reputed to be one of the world's best clinics. *Surely they will help me,* I thought. *I can't wait to feel better!*

After many tests and consultations, a team of physicians in their white lab coats and solemn, professional faces stood over my bed. "I'm sorry, Elizabeth," one of them said. "The damage is permanent."

How can they tell me this?

"Nobody can help you now," the doctor continued gently. "Somehow, you'll have to learn to live with this."

He kept on talking, but his voice receded as darkness flooded in. *How could I live with pain so intense that my whole body shook?* I was only thirty-nine years old, happy, and fulfilled. Life held so much promise. Didn't God say He wanted to use me?

I felt like crying out like the psalmist, "Why, Lord, do you stand far off? Why do you hide yourself in times of trouble?"[17]

I felt Ditmar's grip on my hand. After the doctors left, he turned to me and said, "Honey, don't give up. We'll call upon God and His people to pray. Remember how many times God has already healed you, even as a child."

Yes, Jesus can heal every sickness. His Word says so. The same power that raised Jesus from the dead dwells in me. I am not dead yet, so I have an even better chance to be raised from my sickbed.

I decided to cling to that psalm, for it spoke louder than the pain that tried to block out the reason. Over and over, I repeated God's words until, deep within me, His truth seemed to shout back at the pain and darkness.

In the Bible, I read, "And God is faithful; he will not let you be tempted beyond what you can bear,"[18] but often I felt like He pushed me to the edge.

A week later, a kind nurse invited Ditmar and me to live on her family's farm not far from the hospital. My weight had dropped drastically, and she hoped that fresh milk, eggs, and home-baked bread would restore my strength and hopefully lift my mood as well.

The gloomy, gray November days shrouded not only the landscape but also my soul. Depression had a stranglehold on me. Nothing, not even a crackling fire in the fireplace, could lift my mood.

An early winter chill had settled over the Minnesota hills. I sat wrapped in a blanket, staring out the window at tiny, hard snow crystals hurtling through the air, driven by a sharp wind. In a mindless daze, I watched a herd of cows move as one, in an undulating clump, toward home. But then I noticed, far behind them in the field, one cow standing still with her head lowered.

Why is she staying behind? I wondered. My curiosity piqued, I got up to look through a pair of binoculars. The cow came into view, and then, to my amazement, I saw a newborn calf lying in the grass beside its mother.

"Elizabeth, that cow is just an animal, yet she will not leave her little one. Do you think I would ever leave you alone?"

Tears blurred my vision, and I put down the binoculars. I thought of the Bible verse: "Can a mother forget the baby at her breast and have no compassion on the child she has borne? Though she may forget, I will not forget you!"[19]

I was not alone! God was with me. This thought gave me enough strength to move ahead, even if just for one more day. Still, I pleaded with Ditmar, "Don't ever leave me. I don't trust myself. I wish I weren't afraid, but the truth is: I am very much afraid."

How long would God leave me in "the valley of the shadow of death"?[20]

FLATS AND UNANSWERED QUESTIONS

"This procedure might erase the pain," the specialist said.
"But it might also make it worse."

Our friend wrote to us about a renowned specialist in California who might help me, so we took a flight to seek further medical help there.

"This procedure might erase the pain," the specialist said. "But it might also make it worse."

Desperate for relief, I signed the papers: I was willing to take the risk. As I lay on the table, I was not afraid. I knew nothing could be worse than what I had already experienced. Help was on the way.

But when the doctor injected a local anesthetic into my chest, my heart failed! They put me on a heart machine and kept me alive, but I could not walk after that. I'd lost my balance.

When I looked into the mirror, I gasped. The left side of my face was paralyzed! My lip drooped into an ugly grin, with drool running down. As I stared at my lopsided face, I thought, *Lord, Your Word says You made me beautiful, but this is not a pretty sight!*

I thought of Job who experienced blow upon blow, and I wondered how he could still say, "Though he slay me, yet will I hope in him."[21]

"Almighty God," I prayed, "how much longer will You let the enemy torment me? He has been after me since my childhood! Please, tell me, God, will there ever be an end? How much more do you think I can take? Even cows cry out when hungry or hurt, so don't expect me to keep quiet during this time. It is just too much…."

There were many more mirror-monologues like that one. Often I had to choose: would I listen to Satan's lies or cling to God's Word? Satan would whisper to me, "God doesn't care." He wanted to fill my heart with fear.

So I clung for dear life to Scriptures such as: "He was pierced for our transgressions, he was crushed for our iniquities; the punishment that brought us peace was on him, and by his wounds, we are healed."[22] Over the years, this has become one of my favorite Scriptures.

Like Job, I also had friends who made my suffering worse. Some told me that God was punishing me for some hidden sin. *Why would He punish? Did He not pay a high enough price as He was bruised and wounded?* Trying to find the cause for suffering is a centuries-old debate, but you don't want theological debates when you are hurting.

In the Bible book of Job, I read: "The Lord said to Satan, 'Very well, then, he is in your hands; but you must spare his life.'"[23] Before Satan could attack Job, he had to ask permission. And God gave it to him, but with a condition: so far and no further. So it wasn't Satan but God who was in charge. It relieved me tremendously: I was in God's hands. *But also, I want a divine encounter with You, Lord.*

I drew strength from this quote found in the Quest Study Bible: "Still, many unanswered questions remained. Only God knows why, in Job's case, dozens of bystanders had to die in the unfolding drama between Satan and God. We struggle with the fact that some who are righteous have short, tragic lives, while others who are wicked enjoy wealth and a long life. One thing we can affirm, however: what seems unfair in this life will be made right in eternity."[24]

As long as we live in this fallen world, sin and sickness will be our enemy. As a result of man's sin came death, sorrow, disaster, pain, suffering, and disappointment. Death is normal, but it's not natural. We never get used to it; we were not created to experience it.

Why did God allow me to go through this fiery trial? It remained a mystery to me. Despite intense suffering, God fulfilled His higher plan for Job. One day it would be my testimony, too. In the meantime, it helped me to know God was with me, and He has the last word.

So I decided to trust Him. All that I could do now was look to Jesus on the cross, see Him beaten and bruised. I was ready to receive my healing and wholeness from Him.

I found it difficult to sleep at night. I looked forward to the mornings because then I had less temptation to wrestle with my painful thoughts. I'd sit on the edge of my bed, gathering strength to try and stand up.

"This is the day the Lord has made"—I would quote a scripture—"We will rejoice and be glad in it."[25] I repeated these words every morning through tears. Though my body cried out for rest, I dared not stay in bed. I did not want to give in to pain and depression.

A few days after this last visit, we returned home. As we were preparing to land at the Frankfurt airport, I looked out the window at the familiar landscape below. *How will I make it with this pain?*

"In quietness and trust is your strength,"[26] God seemed to be saying.

I did not realize then what a blessing this Scripture would be to me in the years ahead.

One day I steadied myself against the kitchen sink, watching my neighbors mop their front steps. "Lord, I came to Germany to serve You," I complained, "and I can't even get out and chat with my neighbors."

"Do you want to be used by Me in this country?" He asked.

"Yes, Lord," I answered.

"Then trust Me."

I would trust Him—for a little while. It was a constant struggle between self-pity and trust. One morning Olga Olsson dropped by. She let me pour it all out, then said, "You're in a grieving process, Elizabeth. It's okay to ask questions. Your life has a purpose. Even though, at the moment, you can't see it. Suffering is a high calling, and God knows He can trust you with such an assignment. You know, people need to see how a godly person suffers." She encouraged me to be authentic and not ashamed of my feelings.

The next morning there was a new symptom: my teeth were tightly clenched together. A muscle spasm had locked my jaw. I could not open my mouth, not even to speak or eat. Fear swept over me, and tears sprang to my eyes.

A sudden resolution rose within me. My mouth may be locked shut, but I still have two hands and two feet. I will praise God with them: I will dance before the Lord with all my strength. Feeling sheepish, I closed the drapes so the neighbors wouldn't see me. Then I shuffled my feet and clapped my hands. All morning, I danced before the Lord. About noon, my jaws unlocked, and I told the Lord I would never stop praising Him. That day, praise also became part of my armor. I promised the Lord that, from then on, I would not concentrate on what was wrong with my body but on what was right.

OLD TENNIES AND A NEW IDEA

I looked over the railing at the rushing water below.
"Jump," an evil voice seemed to say.

It was spring, and the beauty of God's creation beckoned me toward a new life. One day, I put on my old tennis shoes and went outside. I walked along a path by the river and into the woods. The trees were cloaked in green again, and little white flowers covered the meadows. The air was fresh, and the birds were singing their morning songs. The sounds, sights, and smells of new life were returning to the forest.

The path led across a little wooden bridge. I paused and looked over the railing at the rushing water below.

"Jump," an evil voice seemed to say. "A shortcut to get rid of the pain, once and for all."

I looked down. *No, the water is too shallow.*

Then that voice replied: "There is a rock. You will hit your head on it, and then it will be over."

Immediately, I recognized the source of the thought: The one who had tempted Jesus to jump from the temple roof was now tempting me to jump. I had just that morning read that in Matthew 4.

"God has given me life," I said out loud.

Tears flowed freely as I stood on the bridge, not caring who might see me. Somehow the discouragement lifted, and a sense of God's presence returned to me. Then deep in my heart, it seemed the Lord showed me the pain of the women in Europe. Yes, tall white steeples, fairy-tale homes with window boxes loaded with blossoms, and white-washed picket fences surrounded me. But behind the well-swept steps, locked doors, and stylish clothes were women in pain.

"Elizabeth," God whispered to my heart, "on the outside, everything looks beautiful and in order, but thousands of women feel like you today. Their pain may be physical or emotional, yet it is still pain, whether it's sickness, loneliness, or another difficulty."

"I want to help, Lord. But what can I do? I am hurting badly myself. Sometimes I wonder how I'll make it to tomorrow."

"Are you afraid of today?"

"No, not too much," I said. "Today, I will make it somehow—with Your help."

"Then leave tomorrow with Me."

I thought of Jesus' words: "Therefore do not worry about tomorrow, for tomorrow will worry about itself. Each day has enough trouble of its own."[27] Jesus seemed to be saying I shouldn't borrow worry from tomorrow.

Looking into the future had always brought fear to me.

"Yes, Lord, I know that all my tomorrows belong to You," I said. "I want to learn to live one day at a time."

It was difficult for me because I'm a visionary. Even as a child, I had my agendas and dreams for the future. But now, I realized that I'd have to learn to walk in the present for me not to fret about the future. To seize *this day* for God's glory! Then tears streamed down my face while I walked along the path.

I remembered that the psalmist said God has "collected all my tears" in a bottle.[28] "My bottle is overflowing already," I reminded God. "Why are You collecting tears anyway?" I walked silently for a while longer. "Or is it true that tears can be like healing waters or the best words the heart can speak? But You promised that, someday, there would be no more tears, and You would wipe them from my eyes."

I waited, and this Scripture came to mind: "Now faith is confidence in what we hope for and assurance about what we do not see."[29] I determined that, as the heroes of faith, I would keep hoping in God. "Teach me how to live like this," I prayed.

During this morning walk in the countryside, I had dynamically experienced the presence of the living God. "Lord, I want Your presence even more than I want my healing," I said. And I meant those words with all my heart.

That day on the bridge, a vision was born in my heart: To start a magazine for women. *When I read stories of other women and how God has brought strength and comfort to them in their pain, I'm so encouraged,* I thought. *Maybe I could tell these stories in a magazine.*

The thought took my breath away: it seemed the right thing to do.

So there, on a bridge over my troubled waters, *Lydia*, a Christian magazine for women, was born.

Just as the world was coming back to life after a cold, barren winter, I felt new life pulsing through me. Excitement stirred my soul. But when I thought of the practical details of starting a magazine, I prayed, "Lord, isn't there somebody more qualified to do this job? How can I even begin to start such a project when it takes all my strength just to get out of bed each day?"

"Trust me."

"Lord, why is it so hard to obey those two little words?" I said. But in my heart, I determined I would trust Him.

I didn't tell Ditmar about my vision. Just as in a gestation period, I felt it needed more time.

Spring turned to summer, and then fall, and finally, it was time for me to share this magazine idea with my husband.

When I told Ditmar about it, he was enthusiastic. "You need to approach some well-known publishers with the vision," he said.

When I did, their response baffled me.

"It won't survive," one publisher said. He told me that the largest German Christian magazine had garnered only ten thousand subscribers in eight years. Consequently, it had to be subsidized. "How can you expect a Christian women's magazine to survive?" he asked. When I looked crestfallen, he added, "We just don't have many Christians in this country." Then he told me that a major Christian publisher had just done a survey with a large, well-known secular publisher of magazines and concluded that there was no market for a Christian women's magazine.

Another publisher said, "Do you know what it takes to run a magazine?" He shook his head in disbelief. "Where will you get the resources?"

Yes, I felt like David facing Goliath. I went straight home to my little attic room, where I often did my praying. "Lord, I don't need to repeat what they told me today. You heard it all," I said aloud.

As I paced the room and praised God for Who He was, suddenly I felt enveloped with comfort and peace.

Then I heard a still, small voice in my heart. "What do you want Me to do for you?" So many longings flooded my mind.

I could ask Him for a child: Ditmar and I had been married for thirteen years and still had no child.

I could ask Him for pain-free days. Yes, life would be much more comfortable then.

But, no! As the ageless words flashed through my mind, "Ask me, and I will make the nations your inheritance,"[30] I knew what I would ask.

"Give me ten thousand women," I said.

I sensed God had heard my prayer.

"Lord, I am so overwhelmed that You have chosen me for this job of starting a women's magazine," I said. "Who am I? The least qualified of all women. I feel like Ruth in the Bible before Boaz as she dropped to her knees…How does this happen that you should pick me…a foreigner?"[31]

"What gift can I bring You? All I can give You is my past, with its many wounds and scars. If You want that, You can have it. I will tell readers of Your unmerited grace to me. I will bring them a message of hope. I will do this fearlessly and unashamedly."

I knew it would be a challenge to find ten thousand readers for a Christian women's magazine. As one publisher had warned me: less than 2 percent of Germans claim to be born-again Christians. Also, I had no experience in putting together a quality magazine.

But my husband and I continued to believe in the vision God had given me.

BIGGER THAN MY DREAM

*We were soon inundated with amazing stories
of God's goodness.*

A year later, we founded the independent *Lydia* publishing house. We had only a thousand marks (about six hundred American dollars), which I had saved from my household money. I began gathering inspirational stories I had heard or read that had been a blessing to me. I studied other magazines to understand what they were doing and why it was appealing—both visually and in content. I believe my childhood eye for fashion and a penchant for writing stories (in the dirt or the snow) helped me now. How amazing to see these two childhood dreams meld and become useful for *Lydia*!

We are often asked why we chose the name *Lydia*. In Germany, women's magazines typically have the name of a woman in the title. (Example: Brigitte, Petra, Lisa, etc.) In searching for a name for the magazine, we came up with a long list. Still, the decision was relatively easy. Acts 16 in the Bible states that Lydia, a woman, was the first Christian in Europe. Her values perfectly fit our concept for the magazine—an open heart for God, an available home for people in need, a free hand to pass on the Good News.

"Lord, I picture young women facing challenges bigger than themselves," I prayed. "They have physical, emotional, and spiritual pain, as well as family problems. I want them to know that they can trust You because You are worthy. I want them to see You like a good Father who loves them. I want to encourage them to find beauty in small things that will give them daily strength and joy."

Ditmar, a former banker who had a natural business sense, oversaw the magazine's production and budget. He managed the books and helped make deals with printers for publication. He did all this in addition to his continuing role as a director of a successful Distance Education University that had hundreds of students. We found a graphic artist to help with the design and layout, and later on, we hired a secretary. I didn't know how many staff people we would need to pull this off, but my passion for encouraging other suffering sojourners outweighed my inexperience. Before we knew it, we were ready to send our first issue to the printer. We had no idea what the public response would be.

Later, in one of my editor's notes, "Ganz persoenlich," I told the story of how *Lydia* was born out of pain. And I encouraged the readers to pray and to send us their God-stories.

Here is one of the early stories I wrote to elicit our readers to join us:

> A fidgety little boy in church pulled on his too-tight collar and stared at the lady's big hat in front of him. Trying not to incur his mother's wrath by wiggling too much, he let his big brown eyes wander around the sanctuary. That was far more interesting than the sermon, which he couldn't understand anyway. *When would it finally be over?*
>
> The young boy's eyes fixed on a stained-glass window, and he became enchanted by the beautiful colors. He wondered silently, *Why do these people's faces radiate with joy and shine like jewels when everyone sitting around me in these pews looks so stern and lonely?*
>
> "Mommy," he tried to whisper. But young, antsy boys do not know how to do that very well. "Who are

those people in the windows?"

"Saints," she snapped back. "Now be quiet."

The next day in religion class, the teacher asked, "Can someone describe a saint to me?"

The young boy excitedly waved his hand. "I can, I can."

"Yes, Tobias," the teacher said, "please explain it to us."

"They are colorful and transparent, and the sun shines through them," he said.

"And how do you know that?" the teacher asked.

"I saw them yesterday in the church's stained-glass windows," he said.

After telling this little story, I encouraged the readers to submit their stories. I told them: Your stories can be full of laughter or sadness. They can describe how you had a unique encounter with Jesus in ordinary (or extraordinary) moments of life. But the article must have these qualities: a theme that captures your heart, that is colorful and transparent.

We wanted honest stories that showed the reality of the struggle, with hope in the midst. We wanted to print stories that showed how Jesus was shining through their lives—how He was leading and giving strength—or how His presence brought them comfort, joy, and healing of the heart.

I was overwhelmed by the responses! The fantastic stories of God's goodness soon inundated us. Hundreds of stories! Heart-warming, heart-healing, and heart-changing stories. I never thought that one day I would be part of God's incredible stories He was carving into human lives; that I would be privileged to publish them.

Through the stories, I realized that spiritual sensitivity is one of the greatest gifts that suffering offers.

When I was a young girl, I had dreamed of writing my poems and stories; now, I was encouraging others to do so. "Lord, it's not exactly what I dreamed, but I am so grateful Your plan was bigger than mine. Thank You for helping me pursue it with passion and purpose."

We also wanted readers to promote the magazine themselves by telling their friends who would tell other friends. Frankly, we didn't have any money for marketing and advertising. We believed that if our readers were contributors, the magazine would feel accessible to the "average" woman struggling to make faith relevant to everyday living.

Readers' stories were pouring in by the hundreds, and I spent hours skimming them for jewels shining through the text. So many stories were touching, bringing tears or laughter. Some challenged us to greater faith and trust in God. As I read them, my heart resounded with the writers' struggles and triumphs—and I found myself worshiping God. I discovered some very talented housewives, who had never written before, but who had a remarkable writing aptitude. It was a pleasure to print their stories and encourage them to develop their craft. Today, several have written books and become well-known authors.

As I tried to promote *Lydia*, I looked for opportunities to speak at women's meetings. I wanted to share the story and the hope that we offered our readers. Today I am glad for everybody who missed my first presentation!

Let me tell you about it. I was at a women's retreat to introduce *Lydia* to a group of ladies. The night before the presentation, an alluring buffet was spread out for us, and I helped myself to generous portions. Either the food didn't agree with me, or it was tainted: I spent the whole night throwing up in the bathroom. Early the next morning, my friend called Ditmar to come to pick me up.

When he arrived, I staggered past some women standing outside in the fresh spring air, awaiting breakfast. Some of them waved at me with deep empathy written all over their faces. I lifted my hand to wave a gracious good-bye, but all of a sudden, I retched violently, and the leftovers of last night's feast came flying out of my mouth.

My girlfriend tried to contain her laughter, but it burst forth. I didn't know whether to laugh or cry, but then the hilarity of it all gripped me, and I also doubled over with laughter.

"So, this is the first *Lydia* presentation." I chuckled. "I guess I'm to learn that the show is not about me." It seemed that the frailty of my body had overruled my plans.

Taking a giant leap of faith, we printed ten thousand copies of the first *Lydia* issue in the spring of 1986. Within a few weeks, they were all gone, snatched up by eager women. So we printed eight thousand more, and when they, too, were gone, we made plans to begin regular production. By the end of the first year, the quarterly *Lydia* magazine had a regular print run of ten thousand!

Grateful letters came pouring into the office. Women were telling us, "This is our magazine." Along with the letters came requests for me to speak at various meetings around the country. It was wonderful to meet with women from diverse backgrounds—all of us finding community in the similarities of our struggles as women.

However, traveling did take its toll on my weak body since I was still suffering from a lot of pain. Often I reminded myself, *In quietness will be my strength.* Even though it was difficult, I needed to learn to say no to many invitations. As someone encouraged me in a card: "To get to the great Yes, you need to say a lot of Nos."

Then one day, we encountered a new pain: Paul Williscroft passed away. Soon Emma Decker's health began to fail. Ditmar and I had been taking care of her affairs, as she was eighty-three years old and had no relatives to help her. She had been a single missionary in China for many years, and when China closed its borders, she had made Germany her home.

One evening we dropped by to see her, something we did as often as we could. We found her sitting in her armchair. "Would you please read Psalm 23 to me?" she asked. (She was no longer able to see well.)

When Ditmar finished reading, he looked at her and said, "Please bless us, Tante Decker." We both knelt before her. She put one hand on me and the other hand on Ditmar, then prayed a blessing over us.

The following day, Tante Decker went to heaven, the place she had longed for so much.

As we buried our heroes of faith, we felt like orphans.

WINGED FEET

When you live with a passionate faith,
no experience is wasted.

"At last, I found answers that apply to my personal life,"
a *Lydia* reader wrote us. "I found Jesus and gave Him my
life. The articles build me up, make me laugh, move me
to tears, and strengthen me. *Lydia* is a real friend."

I could hardly describe the joy I felt when I read notes like that. After one year, *Lydia* was reaching about ten thousand women, and our
mailbox was overflowing with letters each month.

Many women told us how their lives changed because the stories had inspired them and given them new perspectives. Numerous
readers explained how *Lydia* helped them through a time of sickness.
"When I was very ill with depression, a friend brought *Lydia* to me
in the hospital," one woman wrote. "When I read it, I realized how
much Jesus loves me. He didn't just die for my sins. He also wants to
heal me."

An older lady wrote, "How I wish I could have read a magazine
like this in my younger years. It would have kept me from a lot of pain,
and I would have raised my children differently."

It overwhelmed me when we received announcements of a baby's
birth with the remark, "We named our little girl Lydia. Thank you for
showing us when life actually begins." As I read these letters, I would
remember the words of Isaiah: "'Sing, barren woman, you who never
bore a child; burst into song, shout for joy, you who were never in la-

bor; because more are the children of the desolate woman than of her who has a husband,' says the Lord."[32] How true this was for me!

My teenage abortion often crossed my mind as I read these letters, and I couldn't help but grieve once again. Yes, I lost my precious baby, but many women gained theirs due to my story. I asked myself, *Would I have stood up so passionately for pro-life if I hadn't experienced that abortion?* George Mueller, a man who lived his entire life in the light of his passionate faith for Jesus, once said, "In a thousand trials, it is not five hundred of them that work 'for the good' of the believer, but nine hundred and ninety-nine, plus one."[33] That means no disaster, no failures of mine can keep Him from turning the events of my life into something worthwhile.

Don't misunderstand me, though. Abortion is not right. I do not believe it was God's plan for my life. Due to my own choices to befriend those with values opposing mine, I put myself in a precarious position at the risk of fleeing my country with a man I didn't know. The resulting baby, though, was not evil. I grieve when I think of that precious child, not given a chance for life. But when I learned the truth—that life begins at the moment of conception—that truth instilled in me a life-long passion for helping protect these precious little ones. By God's amazing grace, He has chosen to redeem that experience and bring good out of it when I can share it with others who are in or have gone through a similar experience.

I've found out that when you live out a passionate faith, no experience is wasted. Young couples often shared their hearts with Ditmar and me about the pain of infertility. We understood their pain, and we prayed for them with passion because we have been, and still are, walking a mile in those shoes. When some miraculously did welcome little ones—whether through childbirth or adoption—into their hearts and homes, tears of joy flowed down our cheeks as we received the honor of celebrating with them.

What excited us most was that people who would not enter a church were picking up the magazine and reading it. Just as we had hoped, many faithful readers were passing on the magazine to their relatives, coworkers, and friends who said they weren't very interested in God. We were always delighted to hear the stunning results.

One subscriber handed out *Lydia* to her neighbors and later reported: "An eighty-nine-year-old woman, who had left the institutional church after her confirmation as a teenager, returned to God." She concluded her letter by saying, "Who knows how many women will thank you in heaven because *Lydia* has shown them their way back to Jesus?"

Such a comment always made me whisper a prayer: "Help me, Lord Jesus, always to recall how graciously You welcomed me back to Yourself. I want to help others who are making their way back to You one timid step at a time. Help me to love a prodigal world, so it may come home to Your heart where there is never-ending music, feasting, and dancing."

Ines, another reader, wrote:

> I was an active and enthusiastic staff member of a Protestant State Church in our village. During our first staff retreat, my philosophy about heaven collapsed like a house of cards. The speaker said that one does not reach heaven because of good deeds, but through accepting Christ as one's Savior.
>
> *How absurd*, I thought. A few days later, I was sitting at a "Pro Christ" rally (an evangelistic outreach Billy Graham started). That evening, the sermon was on eternity, namely heaven, followed by an altar call to "come to the front and get saved."
>
> I didn't go to the front; I was an active church staff member, after all, and didn't need salvation. My pride wouldn't let me admit that.
>
> A few days later, I was sitting on a train. In my bag was a *Lydia* magazine that my mom had given me. I flipped it open, and my eyes landed—you guessed it!— on an article about heaven. My heart began to beat faster.

> After I read the article (in every issue of *Lydia*, we have
> a salvation prayer that people can follow), I was ready to
> entrust my life to Jesus, but the train was full of people,
> and I couldn't say a prayer in front of a crowd. Still, I felt
> an urgency. It was my time for a change. So, I grabbed
> the magazine and fled to the restroom. There I gave my
> life to Jesus. Imagine, in the restroom with help from
> *Lydia*!

Today Ines is a beautiful young woman who works full-time for God and is leading others to Christ.

When I read her letter, all I could say was, "Yes, Lord. It is my purpose in life: to tell others about You. Help me always to do that with passion." I felt like the woman in the Bible who, when she found a lost coin, shouted, "Celebrate with me! I found my lost coin." The Bible tells us about the angels in heaven also celebrating: "Count on it—that's the kind of party God's angels throw every time one lost soul turns to God."[34]

"Oh Lord, I can just imagine how many parties You are throwing in heaven because women have found You through reading *Lydia* magazine," my heart rejoiced.

As the magazine was born, my first thought was for Christian women to be encouraged by it. Soon I discovered God had an even greater plan: He desired to have a relationship with His creation, and the magazine served as an invitation for that.

Many people today only associate Germany with Hitler and the Holocaust. However, Germany was also the country where the Reformation was born, as Martin Luther discovered the central truth of Scripture: "The just shall live by faith" and pinned his 95 Theses on a church door in Wittenberg. Johannes Gutenberg, who invented the first printing press, printed the Bible that Martin Luther had translated into a common tongue. He worked from Germany but traveled the world.

German revivals changed the globe, such as the Moravian one under Nikolas Ludwig of Zinzendorf in the eighteenth century. As a result, the Moravians sent missionaries to many nations. Some of them made a deep impression on an Anglican priest named John Wesley, leading to the revival that turned England upside down. He later traveled to America and ultimately stirred the Finney revival, followed by the Holiness revival. The Moravians also inspired William Carey, who has been called the "father of Protestant missions." He was impressed by the Moravian's radical obedience to the Great Commission. Some even sold themselves into slavery to take the gospel to the Caribbean. Their cry was, "May the Lamb receive the reward for His suffering."

Yet, in between the eighteenth century and today, something has directly influenced the younger generations. It is heartbreaking to see that a large percentage of people now say they do not even believe in God. It inspired our hearts to bring the Good News: "For God so loved the world that He gave His only begotten Son, that whoever believes in Him should not perish but have everlasting life."[35]

Being the bearer of such magnificent, life-transforming news gives wings to my often-tired feet.

SHOES OF PEACE AND GOD'S PROTECTION

Don't expect that everybody
will celebrate your success.

Not all the responses to *Lydia* were positive, however. One woman returned the magazine ripped to pieces in the same envelope in which she had received it.

Even in some Christian circles, *Lydia* was not welcome, and they let us know about it. It hurt when they rejected the magazine. But God gently reminded me that Christians around the world suffer for His sake.

What we found most challenging was when others wanted this blessing for themselves. We often wondered what to do. God challenged us through friends who asked us, "Are you going to quit because of opposition? Are you going to live cautiously or courageously?" We determined to keep obeying God's call until He told us to move on to another field of service.

I learned quickly: *Don't expect that everybody will celebrate your success. But despite opposition, you have to persevere in God's calling. You have to determine to hold on to the task God has given you to do, no matter what others say and do.*

Realizing I needed protection, I learned to daily put on the armor of God as the book of Ephesians tells us to do:

- The Belt of Truth: *I will not be a victim of Satan's lies.*
- The Breastplate of Righteousness: *I'm protected under the blood of Jesus.*

- The Shoes of Peace: *Yes, I love to spread the Good News of the gospel.*
- The Shield of Faith: *I will not be vulnerable to spiritual defeat.*
- The Helmet of Salvation: *I will keep my mind focused on His promises.*
- The Sword of the Spirit: *Yes, I will take God's Word, my two-edged sword, and fight the good fight of faith.*

I noticed with great interest that all the other armor pieces were for our protection; this one was for advancing the kingdom of God.[36]

Throughout the years, God has provided dedicated staff members who have carried the ministry with compassion.

In choosing staff, we also experienced some failures by not matching the gift with the task. What happened was that we put a maintainer in a promoter position. We delayed facing the problem, and as a result, we experienced what Dr. Henry Cloud states in his book titled *Integrity*. "We can do the hard work of facing a problem and making the necessary changes to resolve it, and then we will enjoy the easy road of having things right. Or, we can take the easy road first and avoid fixing the problem. Then as sure as the sun will come up tomorrow, the hard life will follow. And it will last a lot longer and will be a lot harder than if we had chosen the hard way first."[37]

Through this experience, we reflected and were ready to learn and evaluate. We hope that our painful experience will help others. The school of life offers many challenging courses, some we sign up for, and others we find ourselves in unexpectedly.

I'm also profoundly grateful for the wealth of wisdom offered us by our many authors. Each is an inspiration in her own way. My respect also goes out to our *Lydia* readers, who not only buy the magazine for themselves but give it to others. Some have been doing this for over thirty-four years.

"How, Lord, can I reach more women?" I wondered, "Lord, You are the editor-in-chief of *Lydia*. You know what these women need better than I do. Please, teach me; I want to learn."

In one of our prayer letters, I mentioned how much I like to edit with a pencil. I told my childhood story of when I had just one pencil for the whole school year. I also told our readers that writing with a pencil took less effort and was more comfortable on my hand. Several weeks later, an older lady sent me 365 pencils—one for each day of the year! I thought of Mother Teresa's comment about being "a little pencil in the hands of a writing God who is sending a love letter to the world."

Like her, my heart's desire is to be a pencil in God's hand to write His stories.

FAITH-FILLED SHOES
AND SPREADING THE WORD

"Ask of me, and I will make the nations your inheritance."

In other European countries, Christian women saw copies of *Lydia* and were motivated to start a similar journal in their own language. Many people began contacting us for help and advice. The first foreign magazine we assisted was a French magazine. Soon after that, the Dutch *Eva* was born, and the publisher said *Lydia* had inspired them.

It seemed odd that a young magazine was helping to give birth to new magazines. Sometimes we barely knew what we were doing; we hardly felt equipped to help others. But we tried to share what little we knew. I always found it amazing that we didn't have to master something before we could help others.

Thankfully, God sent us help from Chicago in the form of Sharon Mumper, a passionate magazine professional. She became my consultant and coach. She was a tremendous blessing.

After two years with us in Germany, Sharon relocated to Vienna and founded Magazine Training International (MTI), which coaches and mentors people on how to start a Christian magazine—and make sure it survives.

Ditmar and I continued to make ministry trips to Romania. After the Iron Curtain tumbled down, the misery caused by the long years of communism troubled me. Desperate eyes of children living on the street met mine. Visiting an orphanage was heart-rending.

"Please, take me home," a little girl pleaded while she held on to my leg.

I wish I could have taken all those children home with me! Even more, I knew there were hundreds and thousands of other children who were being aborted before they were even given a chance to live.

Seeing the physical, social, and spiritual needs in the country moved my heart, and a new dream grew within me: *What if we could publish* Lydia *in the Romanian language?*

Ditmar endorsed my idea enthusiastically. He, too, had a heart for Romania, stemming back to his college days when he had smuggled Bibles, clothing, and food to the people there. But he reminded me: "We cannot decide this on our own. We need to ask our board."

"God, please show me whether this is your will or just my idea. I need to know before I present it to the board," I prayed.

Almost a year later, the day came when I was supposed to present the expansion of *Lydia* to the board. But I still hadn't clearly heard from God. So I spent the day praying and fasting: "God, You see the great need of the women in Romania! Surely they could use some encouragement. What do You think?" Then I continued to explain the situation to God, as though He didn't already know it. "Remember, God, that the few copies of the Bible that were smuggled into the country before the fall of communism belonged to men, not women."

As the clock was ticking and the time for our meeting came closer, my shoulders tightened: I still had no answer from God. On an impulse, I looked up the verse God had given me when we founded *Lydia*. "Ask me, and I will make the nations your inheritance."[38] As I read that verse again, I noticed one little letter I had overlooked before.

"There is an 's' after nation!" I exclaimed with surprise. "That means God wants to reach multiple nations with multiple languages!"

An hour later, I presented the idea to our board.

They wished me God's blessings yet did not share my excitement. "You do not have the money for the project," they said. "How will you pay for it?"

Good question. How would we finance the Romanian *Lydia*? I had no answer. Too often, money seemed to be the predominant question.

For the next six months, I went on many prayer-walks through the forest and fields, pleading with God to show me where I could get the money.

"Did I get it right?" I asked again and again. "Nations is plural, right?"

One day as I was walking past a herd of cattle, I recalled what God said in Scripture: "Every animal of the forest is mine, and the cattle on a thousand hills."[39]

Interesting how cows are always speaking to me! I thought, *First, in my childhood. Then, as I returned as a prodigal daughter and realized, You had more than one fatted calf and were always waiting, arms open wide in welcome, for a celebration. Later, at Mayo Clinic, when You promised You would never leave me nor forsake me. And now again, right here in this field. Maybe the moos would tell me what to do. Perhaps I understand cow language the best!*

I laughed aloud: "Couldn't You sell a few cows, God, and give me the money?"

We had a heart-to-heart talk, God and I, and it seemed that He was saying: "Elizabeth, you keep telling Me what to do. Why don't you tell your readers what is on your heart?"

I had never thought about that. So my staff and I prepared a small, simple, black-and-white brochure in which I explained my vision: why we should help women in other countries. I also reminded them how Germany had been a blessing throughout history: Martin Luther translated the Bible into German, Johannes Gutenberg invented the printing process, and German Moravian missionaries sold themselves into slavery to share the gospel. Is it possible that God would want to use us to bless other nations? Couldn't we women play a role in this? Then I explained our need for finances.

We placed the request in the following issue of *Lydia*. The response was amazing! Soon letters from excited women piled up on my desk.

"Yes," many women wrote, "together we can do that!"

One woman from East Germany wrote:

> Please let me explain why I want to help women in
> Romania. I grew up in a so-called "socialist" country. We
> never heard anything about God or faith. I am thirty-
> eight years old, and I did not know anything about the
> healing power of God until I received Lydia. After all
> those years, I entrusted my life to God. At last, I am
> no longer afraid. I came to God like a child. Thanks
> to Lydia, I've had this experience. That's why I want to
> contribute to this project, so that Romanian women,
> who have also lived in a socialist country, will have the
> opportunity to get to know God and the healing power I
> have experienced.

I was stunned by the outpouring of support and how this God-idea seemed to multiply. *Lydia* was helping transform lives, and just like the woman at the well, who dropped her water pot to run and tell the people in her town about Jesus (John 4), our readers were more than ready to share the burden of telling the "nations."

In 1993, we finished the first Romanian issue by translating some articles from the German *Lydia*. We printed the Romanian magazine in Germany because the paper was much cheaper than in the Eastern bloc. We took the issue to the printing company and got another surprising offer: "Why don't you add another language?" an employee suggested. "Considering the minimal additional cost, it would be reasonable. All we'd need to do is change the black plates."

We were still so new to the publishing industry that we didn't even know that was possible. The additional language choice was not difficult: It seemed only natural to choose Hungarian, my heart's language!

The following month, a truck loaded with copies of *Lydia* crossed the border into Hungary and Romania—this time with permission from the governments! With the fall of the Iron Curtain, there was no more need to smuggle. I would have never thought it possible! Once I risked my life to get a small number of teaching materials across the border for a handful of children. Now we could deliver 75,000 copies of this Christian magazine's first issue in Romanian and 25,000 in Hungarian.

Thanks to some contacts in both countries, we distributed the magazines at no cost. It seemed all the denominations wanted the magazine, even some orthodox ones. Statistically, we know more than 500,000 people read the 100,000 copies. One copy would get handed from person to person four to five times. Even today, they pass around the old issues until they fall apart. Sometimes an entire village reads one magazine.

I have always believed in the power of the printed page. I had seen how the communists used printed material to propagate their beliefs. Now we had the opportunity to use the printed page to give women meaning in life, help them grow in their faith, and become better women, mothers, and wives.

Men also thanked us for the new magazine. Pastor Paul Negrut, the Romanian Evangelical Alliance leader, became one of *Lydia's* prominent promoters.

A senator from Romania expressed his appreciation for the magazine and invited us to visit the parliament. *How incredible*, I thought. *Once I was risking my life to cross this border. Now I'm being invited to the parliament.*

The good old days before communism. Mother is sitting next to my favorite Aunt Elizabeth. My oldest sister Edit is standing and Rosie is sitting on Mother's lap.

1963: I was curious to explore the big wide world of the west.

My grandparents, who I loved with all my heart. Grandma awakened my love for stories. With the help of a big, shaggy dog, Grandpa taught me to walk, and later accompanied me when I took my first steps in faith.

Baskets full of malva. Harvest was a tedious task in my childhood. Later, as an adult, I did not mind this work.

Mother and Father with us girls. Back row from left to right: Maria, Edit, Rosie, Elizabeth (me), and Martha. Front row from left to right: Valerija and Erika.

The house where I grew up.

Arriving in Vancouver, Canada, and being welcomed by Ditmar's family for the first time.

As a bride in my wedding gown which I sewed myself.

Our new home in Vancouver, where Ditmar grew up.

Finally in America—which was my life long dream—the land of the free and the home of the brave, with its beautiful palm trees and the Pacific Ocean. Here I experienced a time of testing.

In California we found life long friendships with Anita and Albert Vaters with whom we took trips later. Here we are in Ireland.

Joni Eareckson Tada and Ken Tada, longtime friends. From the start, Ditmar enjoyed lending them his voice as a translator when they were touring Germany. Here we are celebrating Joni's birthday in Frankfurt.

A new stage of life begins in Germany as missionaries. I loved Germany and even their traditional outfits.

A few years later God surprised me and trusted me with Lydia the Christian magazine for women which became the largest Christian magazine in the country.

I spent many hours sorting through stories. Sometimes my little dog Annie sneaked in and wanted to help me.

In 1989 when communism fell and the door opened to Eastern Europe, women were very interested in having a magazine in their own language. I talked to future editors in Moscow at an MTI conference.

We were able to help other magazines get started.

In 1993, on the trip to Romania, I contracted Lyme disease which was discovered very late and my life was in danger. This was the time of my dark valley but God surprised me by sending me a special Christmas gift. (Chapter 28)

I was especially eager to help Eastern European women. In 1993, after communism had fallen, the Romanian Lydia magazine was the first to be born.

At the 25th anniversary celebration, the magazine looks different—as do the readers.

1999: I opened the Hope for Europe Women's Congress in the Frankfurt Festhalle.

10,000 women including representatives from 32 countries attended.

Representatives of the various nations knelt to pray in front of the flags of their homelands, which they brought before the cross.

RUNNING SHOES FOR CHRISTMAS

What drastic measures He takes
to place well-timed gifts in our lives!

After a week in Romania, for some unexplainable reason, my leg started to swell. We packed our things and prepared to head toward Budapest, Hungary. From there, we planned to return home to Germany. But during the night, I became severely ill; I had a foreboding sense that my condition was critical. In the morning, Ditmar decided that we would go to Austria to consult a physician instead of going to a Budapest hospital.

The doctor examined me, then said, "It could be stress-related." He gave me an injection and sent us on our way home to Germany.

During the following weeks, my condition worsened. I went to see another doctor. He couldn't figure out, either, why I was in such pain and had difficulty walking. Water was accumulating in my legs, causing them to swell. A doctor needed to drain fluid from my knee regularly.

In December 1994, my entire body ached, and I couldn't walk anymore. I needed a miracle.

I was now using a wheelchair. Ditmar took me to yet another doctor. Suspecting a severe viral infection, they ran some blood tests.

A few days before Christmas, we discovered the real reason for my pain: I had contracted Lyme disease. A tick must have bitten me while I was walking through the fields in Romania, and the physicians had not discovered it in time to effectively treat it. Six months after the initial infection, the disease had now spread throughout my entire body. I was rushed to the hospital to receive intravenous antibiotics.

"I want to go home for Christmas," I said to the doctor in the hospital.

He was not pleased. "Do you know how serious this is?" he asked. "You don't have much of a chance of living through it."

Still, he let me go home. Our family doctor visited us in our home. He also expressed his deep concern and asked us gently if our affairs and our will were in order.

I told Ditmar, "If Jesus calls me home, please bury me in Germany." We had lived in so many places that I didn't know where my home was. "This is our home by choice," I continued, "and I've come to love it dearly." The Germans were kind to us. We were one of them, and we felt we truly belonged in Germany.

That Christmas, we talked about my funeral, our will, and *Lydia*. I had one more wish: that our staff could bring one *Lydia* magazine and the first book that *Lydia* had published, which was a Christmas book, accompanied by a letter, to each home in our town. I wanted to make sure that everyone had a chance to understand why Jesus was born and why we celebrate Christmas.

As I read Psalm 90 and how the psalmist describes our life on this earth, I thought: *Since I am going to heaven, I want to know more about it.* Ditmar gathered up books about heaven and read to me each evening. I especially loved what Ruth Kopp, MD, said in her book *When Someone You Love is Dying:* "When I face my own death, I believe I will be able to see my father's house beyond the valley of the shadow, and death will be, not the end, but merely the passageway to a new beginning."[40]

It was my hope also. Sometimes I would even dream about heaven. I would glimpse beautiful scenery I had never seen on this earth. Someone was holding my hand, but I could not see the face. I felt so loved as we danced, unfettered, through hills and fields, leaving pain and my wheelchair behind. Then I saw the eyes of numerous women gazing at me, and I woke up.

How wonderful heaven will be, I couldn't help but think, as pain radiated all through my body. *As Revelation says, heaven will be a comfortable home with no tears, no pain, no death. We will dwell in perfect peace with God, free from the burden of sin and suffering.*

I looked at my husband, my sweetheart, and thought of the work with *Lydia*. I prayed, "Lord, someday I will come to You anyway, but could I please stay a little longer here on this earth? There is so much to do. My body is frail, but my spirit is willing."

On Christmas Eve, it was just Ditmar, our sweet little dog, Annie, and me. This year there wasn't a trace of Christmas spirit in our house, not even a strand of tinsel or a nativity scene. But we had each other. Then Ditmar, trying to improve my spirits, handed me a present.

A little while later, I asked him, "Honey, didn't I get a parcel at the beginning of November? Some ladies from Illinois sent it to me, I think." I vividly remembered the brown wrapped box with big letters across the side that proclaimed: *Do not open until Christmas Eve!* I had almost forgotten about it!

Ditmar found the package and handed it to me. As I removed the brown wrapping paper, I saw a shoebox. *Who would be sending me shoes?* I wondered. *Nobody has ever given me shoes as a present.* (Oh, yes, my mother had given me money for shoes, but I'd spent that money instead on buying a pig to feed the children at camp.)

Inside the box was a pair of white running shoes. *How ironic!* I thought. I turned to Ditmar and said, "Running shoes? Who knows whether I will ever walk again?"

While inspecting the shoes, I read aloud the label inside: *Walking shoes.*

Ditmar and I looked at each other and started to cry. Here I was, sitting immobilized in a wheelchair. How ridiculous was a gift of walking shoes?

Or maybe, just maybe, it was a sign of hope. "God, did You send me walking shoes to tell me I will walk again?"

How often we had seen the benevolent and powerful hand of God in our lives. We concluded God must be sending us a message of hope:

I would walk again. We knew we could hold onto God's impeccable timing.

The women who had picked the gift did not know my situation. They had shipped the package surface mail from Illinois at the end of the summer, hoping it would reach us by Christmas.

They must have bought the shoes about the time the tick bit me.

God, however, had not been taken by surprise. He knew, even way back in summer, that I would need a visual reminder of His love to rekindle my hope now. What drastic measures He takes to place well-timed gifts in our lives!

That pair of white walking shoes got a special place next to my bed. Every morning as I looked at them, I was reminded of God's special attention. For a whole year, month after month, these shoes were my only sign of hope, reminding me to believe God's promise: One day, I would walk again!

Even though my legs were not working, my mind was free to work on the magazine. I usually worked from my couch, glad that I had something to distract me from the wrenching pain.

My neighbor lady came to visit from time to time and even brought me a home-cooked meal. One day she asked, "Where are all your Christian friends? I don't see them coming anymore." She smiled as she continued, "We used to call your home 'Mittelstaedt's Hotel' when we saw how many guests were coming and going. But now, hardly anyone comes. Where is God now when you are suffering?"

I shared with her Elie Wiesel's account, from his book *Night*, of an execution in a Nazi concentration camp during World War II. The prisoners were made to watch the hanging of a young boy. As the boy suffered, slowly strangling to death, a prisoner cried out, "Where is God?"

A voice rang out from the crowd: "Right there on the gallows."

"Where is God?" I echoed my neighbor. "He's right here beside my couch. He is suffering with me because He is the perfect Father."

She was quiet for a moment. Head lowered, my neighbor asked, "Did you know I was Hitler Youth?"

"No, I didn't know that," I said.

She merely nodded and left.

I prayed for my neighbor as soon as she left. The story God had brought to mind to share with her stunned me. I worried that I'd offended her. But as our friendship grew, I realized my neighbor was searching for more meaning in life. She was grappling with the pain and guilt of her past. Ditmar and I were able to share with her, her husband, and her father about God's forgiveness, mercy, and grace.

In my search for healing, I read many books on the subject. We prayed daily and asked others to pray for me. I was sure that every prayer on my behalf was like the blow of a hammer. Persistent. Never-ending. The prophet Jeremiah says God's Word is… "like a hammer that breaks a rock in pieces."[41] Ever wonder how a hammer can hit a rock 99 times, but on the 100th blow, it shatters? That's because all the previous blows weakened it.

I worked on daily exercises to strengthen my legs and slowly transitioned from the wheelchair to crutches.

I cannot say why God did not heal me, once and for all, and rid me of facial pain from the dental malpractice. I have experienced long stretches, though, when Lyme disease is dormant.

Through every moment and every life circumstance, God is teaching me to trust Him. One thing I know for sure: I need His help every day, for I could not go through all this alone. God is showing me to stop trying and start trusting.

I have staked my hope, life, passion, and purpose on the God who is always with us. The God who never changes, from generation to generation. "I've pitched my tent in the land of hope…. You've got my feet on the life-path."[42] Each day I find hope and healing in His Word for the next stage of our journey.

WARM BOOTS FOR RUSSIA

As we were ready to leave,
a police officer appeared...

Shortly after communism fell, I made a trip to Russia.

I was traveling alone, and there were not many people to watch at the Moscow Airport. At the passport checkpoint, the officer glanced at me, examined my Canadian passport, then finally stamped it.

I stepped outside the security area and into the airport public area to search the crowd for the gentleman who was to pick me up. They told me that he would be holding a sign with my name on it.

There was nobody.

In a panic, I began thinking: *Can I find a phone? And, even if I do, can I figure out how to use it?*

Finally, way in the back, I saw the sign held up by a young man I'd never met. I let out a deep sigh and walked in his direction. Politely, he introduced himself and helped me with my suitcase.

We trudged through the knee-high snow to his beat-up Russian car. I was glad I had dressed appropriately in warm boots and winter wear. Still, the cold November wind cut through my coat, and I could not wait to jump into the car to escape the chill.

As we were ready to leave, a police officer appeared. He knocked on the window with his baton and motioned the driver to get out. My heart froze. I didn't know if this former communist country would be similar to my own.

My driver complied, and the policeman said something I could not understand.

"You stay here." The young man popped his head back into the car. "I will be back shortly."

He locked the car and followed the policeman.

How long he was gone, I cannot recall, but my teeth were chattering from the cold, and my feet were freezing despite my warm boots. Even worse, fear flustered my heart.

"What was the problem?" I asked when he finally got back in the car.

"Let's not talk about it, please," he said.

Being from a former communist country myself, I understood certain things you don't talk about.

An hour later, after winding through the city's colorless, gray blocks, we arrived at a massive building in the middle of nowhere. The building had few windows and looked like a military base.

Nevertheless, I stepped into the main entry hall and gawked at the colossal airplane hanging from the ceiling. Now, that was an odd decoration for a hotel! My already rattled imagination took over, and I wondered why my driver had brought me here and how I would handle this strange situation. Later that evening, I found out the building wasn't a hotel; it was a Russian Space Research Center.

At the entrance, they wanted to see my passport. I was given a complete security check and then received a security card.

"Never lose this card," the guard told me. "Without this card, you cannot leave the building, nor will you be allowed to come back in."

I was here at the invitation of Magazine Training International (MTI), which provided workshops to teach and encourage people who work for or want to start a Christian magazine in the former Soviet Union. Attendees would receive training in various fields of journalism: writing, editing, graphic design, and business. About fifty-five staff members from twenty-four different magazines had signed up for the three-week conference.

Finally, I saw familiar faces from MTI: Sharon Mumper and other team members welcomed me. I hugged my old friends from NavPress and *Christianity Today*. What relief! What joy! We were all there to teach and encourage Christian journalists to cultivate their dreams and skills in writing, publishing, and testifying to God's truth, even in challenging economic times.

Although most of the seminar participants were men, there were a handful of women as well. I was thrilled to see some young women, like Oxana, who had dreamed of publishing a Christian women's magazine. Although desperately homesick for her young children, Oxana had traveled several hundred miles from another part of Russia to help hone her craft. She stayed through the very last workshop because she wanted to learn everything she could in order to see her vision come to life.

I also met Anna, a redheaded, brave editor of a newspaper high on Russia's northern borders, near the Arctic Circle. She came to the meetings afraid that her newspaper would not survive the many changes that had recently taken place in her country. Anna left the conference with tears of gratitude—thankful for the encouragement she received and full of hope to continue spreading truth in the sparsely populated territory of north Russia.

Some evenings, after an already long, full day of seminars and meetings, these women invited me to their rooms. They always served good Russian tea, accompanied by delicious cookies that they had brought with them. We had a lot of fun talking in different languages, and when we lacked words, we used our hands. The women asked many questions and shared their dreams. I was so glad to hear that a year later, a Christian women's magazine in Russian was on the market.

The third morning, it was my turn to speak to all the participants during the general session. Unfortunately, I struggled with finding the right words, so I shortened my message. Besides, as I looked out over the audience, I was distracted by the faces of some of the men. Their eyes were closed, and their body language communicated that they were not interested in what I had to say. I sensed the familiar tension between men and women that I had faced so often in Eastern Europe. In an audience where age often speaks louder than experience or knowledge, grimaces met my gender and youthful looks. I felt as if the men were screaming their disapproval even in silence, and all I wanted was to end my speech early to escape all the glares.

Just as I gathered my notes to leave, the moderator Sharon, stepped onto the stage and said, "Thank you, Elizabeth. We still have time left for this session, so I'd like to ask you a few questions to help our audience understand more about *Lydia* and your work there."

I was trapped.

"Elizabeth, how large is *Lydia's* circulation?"

Her first question pinpointed what I wanted to leave out intentionally. I did not mention this in my speech because I knew that many editors struggled with their magazines and were happy if their circulation reached figures in the hundreds, let alone thousands. I did not want to discourage them with the high numbers that we had seen.

"The German circulation is about eighty thousand," I said timidly.

Suddenly, the men, as if hit by a jolt of electricity, straightened their backs and sat up in their chairs. I could see several of them leaning forward to listen more intently, staring at me with their heads cocked ever so slightly. I could imagine them asking in disbelief, "What? This woman did that?"

Whispers followed a shifting of posture: "Did you hear that? She said eighty thousand. Imagine eighty thousand. Wow!"

I almost burst out laughing. Now I had their full attention. *How amazing that the answer to this one question has made me respectable in their eyes,* I thought. These traditional, Eastern European men couldn't argue away or ignore results, even if those results were at the hands of a woman!

The women also changed their posture. They had eagerly listened to me throughout my talk. But when they saw the men react to the circulation numbers, I could see a glow upon their faces. They, too, sat up straighter in their chairs, with smiles spreading broadly across their faces. Many women told me afterward how encouraged they were. They said that day gave them the courage to continue pursuing their dreams in what was then a predominately men's world of publishing.

Later, several of the ladies asked me to talk more about the gender issue. "What can a woman do? What is our role in God's plan?" they asked. Many cultural traditions had obscured their understanding of God's will for their lives as women.

So I explained to them what I had gathered from my experience. "God wants male and female to be counterparts, face to face, equals, each unique and different, distinctive in gender but complementary, and each empowered uniquely. God created Eve to answer His admission that 'it is not good for the man to be alone. I will make a helper suitable for him.'[43] He created her as a 'helper'—the same Hebrew word for helper also used by God to describe Himself."

At the end of the MTI conference, I joined a team of teachers on a trip to Red Square in Moscow. The city sparkled under a fresh blanket of snow and a minus fifteen-degree temperature. We walked around, looking in awe at Saint Basil's Cathedral, the Kremlin, and Lenin's Mausoleum.

After taking a look at the Kremlin, we entered the famous Saint Basil Cathedral, named after the Russian Orthodox Saint Basil: "Fool for Christ." As I observed the Orthodox worship service, I noticed a young man kneeling in prayer. His face was creased in concentrated fervor as he silently poured out his heart to God.

After a while, God nudged my heart: "Go talk to him."

"Oh no," I resisted. "I don't know the language."

Repeatedly, I seemed to hear God whisper the same thing to my heart: "This man needs to know that I love him."

As I silently argued with God, telling Him my reasons this wouldn't work, the man stood up.

Finally, I thought, *he's going home, and I'll get rid of this inner struggle.*

But the man walked over to another corner to kiss an icon and pray some more.

At this, I knew all my objections were self-centered. Clearly, God wanted to communicate His love to this man. So I sheepishly asked our guide to be my interpreter. We walked over to the man, and I introduced myself.

Surprised, he told me his name was Vladimir.

I began to ask him questions about Jesus.

I felt another nudge in my heart: "Give him some money" (even though that is not recommended).

Before leaving, I reached into my purse and handed him some money.

Vladimir swallowed hard and lowered his head.

"What's wrong?" I asked.

"I was just praying for help today. That is why I came to church. My family is in such great need. And now—"

Placing my hand on his shabby, thin coat, I looked into his moist eyes. "Vladimir, God is here to tell you He will care for you. I am only here for a moment to show His love. But God will stay with you, and He will never leave you."

Again, those powerful words that had so influenced my life—*I will never leave you*—now influenced young Vladimir's life.

Once outside the church, my tears started to flow. How ironic that, like St. Basil, I also had been looked upon as somewhat of a "fool" for Christ! Some years ago, as I was standing on a bridge in the German countryside, I had sensed the pain of women across Europe. Now I was once more overwhelmed by the lostness of the people wandering around me. "Oh, Jesus, how many in this world, like Vladimir, are searching for God and just need someone to tell them?"

"You have a great privilege, Elizabeth," I sensed God speaking to my heart. "Not even the angels get to share the gospel—I've left that task to humans."

"God," I said, "I want to spread the good news of Your love, forgiveness, and freedom through both the printed and spoken word and with prayers and kindness. Help me to always do so with purpose and passion!"

At that very moment, I sensed a parade of angels in that square, rejoicing with me that Vladimir experienced God's love.

And all it had taken was a fool—a fool who was obedient to God's nudging.

CHAINED FEET IN CROATIA

If we want to do something of great importance,
it often comes with a price-tag.

On my flight back to Frankfurt, I mulled over the rich impressions and snippets of conversations from the past weeks in Moscow.

I could hear God saying clearly, "My harvest is plentiful! Attend to the harvest."

My heart ached for Eastern Europe and the former Soviet republics, and I longed to see more magazines that would spread the good news. *The suffering, rejection, poverty, and illness are severe, but that's still not the worst thing they are suffering,* I thought. *The worst thing is to be without love, without purpose, without hope, and without God.* Repeatedly, I asked the Lord and myself: *How can I make a difference?*

I spent some very restless nights thinking about the many needs of the harvest and how God might use me to help meet those needs. In the wee, still hours of one sleepless night, I thought of all the Christmas stories readers had sent to *Lydia*—way too many for us to use in the magazine. *What if we put them together into a Christmas book? The money from the sale of the books could help fund women's magazines in Eastern Europe.*

My heart pounded with excitement at the possibilities.

The very next day, my staff and I began compiling these unused stories. After collecting and formatting them, I pitched the book to a prominent publisher. He declined, saying, "Christmas books don't sell well. The season is too short. We can't make a profit."

Although I was discouraged, I felt this was a God-given project. I continued to pursue different publishers to take this on. A year later, someone finally agreed to publish the book, and before we knew it, *Ein bisschen beim Stern sitzen (Sitting a Little While by the Star)* was out on the shelves.

None of us could have predicted what happened next, but it was similar to the first edition of *Lydia* that flew off the shelves: the book was a best-seller for months in Germany's Christian book markets. Later on, it was translated into Croatian. We heard that the Catholic priests in Croatia liked the book and used some of its stories to illustrate their sermons. The book was even read on radio and TV, and the Croatian people voted for it to win the Golden Heart award for "Most Inspirational Book." The next year, a Romanian and Hungarian translation followed.

Not only did the Christmas book touch people's hearts, but God also used it to generate funds to create more printed resources to spread the gospel. We followed up the Christmas book with a unique Bible for women—a New Testament with devotional texts written by women for women. It appeared first in German and then in Romanian. We also created a devotional of the "wisdom books" of the Bible: Job, Psalms, Proverbs, Ecclesiastes, and Song of Solomon. It was equally popular and is still the only one of its kind. Other books followed.

It's incredible what God can do, with a little passion and purpose, to turn one tiny seed of an idea into a blossoming ministry.

In December 2006, I received word that the Christmas books could also be given out at a women's prison in Croatia. It was a momentous pronouncement, representing more than a decade of prayer that God would bring healing and salvation to the many wounded women in former Yugoslavia. We all remembered the Balkan war, which started in the early 1990s. At that time in the magazine, we focused on the rape camps and encouraged *Lydia* readers to pray for women to take any action they could.

This time I asked our *Lydia* prayer group to pray specifically for lonely women prisoners. Finally, on December 18, 2006, we were given permission to do an hour program in a prison entitled, "What Is the Purpose of My Life on Earth?"

My sister Maria, who lived in Vukovar, Croatia, and was involved in a humanitarian ministry, was responsible for the paperwork for getting us behind these bars. Although many times she wanted to give up, I kept reminding her: "If we want to do something of great importance, it often comes with a price tag." I'm so glad she stuck with it (with my foreign passport, we felt it would not be wise for me to go into the prison, being a magazine editor).

The morning of the event, while I was praying and reading my Bible, I came upon the words, "I needed clothes and you clothed me, I was sick and you looked after me, I was in prison and you came to visit me."[44] I couldn't believe I was reading these verses now. (I had been reading through Matthew systematically and hadn't been looking for verses that might "fit" a prison ministry.) Although I had read the words many times before, this time, they impacted me differently. I felt like Jesus was saying, "Today, in the prison, you will see Me working."

I sat there, stunned.

After I caught my breath, I picked up the phone and called Maria. "You won't believe what I just read!" I said.

"What?" she asked.

"Listen," I said and reread the verse to her. "Maria, don't be afraid! You are going to see Jesus working today, and I will be praying for you."

"Thank you," she said. Then she added, "I needed to hear that. I would have given up a long time ago if you hadn't been so persistent in encouraging me. Elizabeth, we're seeing a dream come true today!"

I did a lot of pacing the floor that day while waiting for a phone call from Maria. I wanted to hear how it went. Finally, my impatience got the best of me, and I called her. "How was it?"

Maria was so overwhelmed that she had a difficult time expressing herself. After a deep sigh, she said, "It was awesome, Elizabeth. It was more than what we ever dreamed of or asked for. I know God did this, and He deserves the glory."

She took a deep breath, then continued: "More than fifty prisoners came, mostly young women. Their expressions were so demoralized. But as I gazed upon their faces, I did not see murderers. I saw broken young women who had made bad choices early in their lives and were now suffering a maximum-security sentence. Still, they were God's creations, like the rest of us.

After everyone had settled in, there was silence—something we had not expected. It was not a threatening silence; it was a hushed stillness filled with awe. We could sense God was near. What an opportunity we had to tell them about God's forgiveness and love for them! The inmates were so attentive, hanging onto every word. The guards who stood on both sides of the room also listened well."

Visiting the women's prisons with the Good News was a historical event. Since then, we have been granted permission to visit the prison twice a year, and each time the attendance increases, and they ask when we will return. Some women have grown in their faith—for example, Slavica, who completed her prison term and today lives in Bosnia and is involved in a local church.

On every visit, we have an hour program and take some literature such as *The Hiding Place* by Corrie ten Boom, *Joni* by Joni Eareckson Tada, and other valuable books translated into the Croatian language. We also distribute gifts of chocolate, shampoo, or warm socks—something personal to each woman.

STEPPING OUT, DREAMING BIG

*God had so much more in store
than I even asked or dreamed!*

The German *Lydia* and her two offspring publications in Romanian and Hungarian were well underway, even being produced in their respective countries, although the German *Lydia* was still helping financially.

In the summer of 2004, I was invited to be the keynote speaker at the first conference for women's magazines sponsored by MTI. Teams from twenty-three Christian women's magazines, representing twenty-three nations, traveled to Slovakia for a week of seminars and fellowship.

Ditmar traveled with me and gave consultations to many teams as a financial advisor. We enjoyed meeting and talking with the fifty-five editors and publishers throughout the week. Many editors had become dear friends as I had walked with them and helped them pursue their dreams. During the conference, each magazine team gave a ten-minute report. Listening to them humbled me beyond measure: Thirteen of the twenty-three magazines for Christian women had been inspired or helped by *Lydia* magazine.

As the magnitude of *Lydia's* influence hit Ditmar and me, our eyes clouded with tears. Yes, we'd given a lot of advice and financial help throughout the years, but for some reason, we didn't realize the power of it.

Furthermore, we were amazed to hear of the impact many of these magazines were having in their nations. *Lea*, the Bulgarian magazine, initiated a club where they teach journalism to Christians and non-Christians alike. Several Russian editors spoke up against abortion and were watching in amazement how the number of abortions dropped.

We kept hearing many stories of how *Lydia* was building bridges between different denominations in various countries. Again, it struck me: *God had so much more in store than I even asked or dreamed!*

When I was just a little girl sitting at a dilapidated desk in first grade in Yugoslavia and memorizing poems, or writing words in the dust that the wind blew away, who could have known that the wind of the Holy Spirit would someday blow the Word in so many directions? I certainly never dreamed of it. Yes, I somehow knew the printed page could change the world. And yes, even at that tender age, God planted a seed in my heart that took decades to form and come to fruition.

I thought my little dreams were dashed when I could no longer go to school.

I thought they were rerouted when I pursued sewing, and later on, when I smuggled Bibles and children's materials into "closed" countries.

I thought there was no hope for living, much less of being any use in God's kingdom, as I stood on a bridge over troubled waters.

But God had not forgotten the seed He planted so long ago. In every stage of life, He was preparing me and inviting me to pursue the dreams of my heart. From the two thousand doctors' offices and hospitals that carry the magazines to our staff, supporters, and faithful readers, each one of us has done our part for the harvest. And for some reason, God has seen fit to bless.

In 1986, God gave me the promise, "Ask of me, and I will make the nations your inheritance." It was in His heart to touch many nations. God was the One who encouraged me to ask for the souls who are still in darkness—the most significant request I've ever made.

It was a considerable faith risk to request 10,000 women to buy *Lydia*. But twenty years later, for our 2006 anniversary edition of the

German *Lydia*, the circulation was 100,000. We had subscribers in more than 100 countries worldwide, with a readership of half a million. A few extra zeroes are nothing to the God Who gave the dream and Whose heart is in relentless pursuit of a hurting world.

WOMEN FROM ALL WALKS OF LIFE

The task was immense,
and there were so many more qualified than I...

"We need a woman who knows the West and has a heart for the East," Lorry said. "I think you are the one, Elizabeth!"

Lorry Lutz was the leader of the AD2000 and Beyond Woman's Track, the purpose of which was: To be a catalyst for God to unleash the under-utilized resource of women around the world through the power of prayer, encouragement, and training for world evangelization. They wanted to bring leaders from different organizations and denominations together for the sake of the gospel.

Lorry's challenge to lead a women's track at the AD2000 conference in 1991 pulled the carpet out from under my feet. Well, actually, it placed me on the carpet—under my kitchen table, face down, beseeching God.

"Please, God, talk to me!"

This wasn't the first time Lorry had asked me. She was searching for a leader who could bring women from the Eastern and Western European countries together, and she thought I was a good fit. The task was immense, and every time Lorry asked me, I declined.

"There are many women much more qualified than me," I would tell her. "Besides, I have physical limitations…and…and…"

I had plenty of excuses, and Lorry always listened graciously. She also always returned to me with the same request.

So here I was, wrestling with God on the carpet, under the table in my kitchen! Why on earth did I choose such an odd place? Maybe it reminded me of the time when, as a child, I'd sit under the table with my cat while Grandpa read from God's Word.

"Show me, Lord!" I kept praying. "Should I accept this position with its responsibilities?" I had struggled with saying "no" before—doing too many "good things" all at once and exhausting myself. Now I desired to only say "yes" if it was the right thing.

All of a sudden, I heard a voice, and it wasn't God's voice. "Stop it, Elizabeth!" yelled the woman from the apartment underneath mine. I was praying so loud that the older woman living downstairs could hear me through the floor.

"I want to sleep!" she shouted angrily, punctuating each word with a jab of her heavy broomstick against the ceiling.

But how can I stop praying until I hear from God? I thought. *I need to know whether I should take this job.* But I did pray more quietly as I continued, "Is this your will, God?"

Suddenly, God's beautiful peace enveloped my soul. Not a peace that comes when you've figured out all the answers, but one that says, "Don't be afraid. I will be with you."

I grabbed a pencil and began making a list to see how this opportunity fit my calling.

- Women? *Yes, that's been my purpose all along.*
- Encourage? *That's been my passion for years.*
- Printed page? *I can't see how leading a woman's track fits this. Hmmm—two plusses and one minus!*

Challenging women leaders to get together for the sake of the gospel always brought me joy. From experience, I knew finding joy in my work energized me, even in chronic pain.

After more prayerful consideration, I said yes to leading a women's leadership conference.

ELIZABETH MITTELSTAEDT

My first task was to bring together female Christian leaders from all over Europe who belonged to different denominations and organizations. In April of 1993, I asked about forty women from Eastern and Western Europe to join us in Linz, Austria, including Lorry Lutz, AD2000 leader; Robyn Claydon from the Lausanne Committee for World Evangelization; and Ingrid Kern with World Evangelical Fellowship Commission on Women's Concerns. This gathering of women from three major evangelical organizations became known as "Hope for Europe—Women in Leadership."

For the first time, leaders from different countries and denominations spent one entire week together getting to know one another, learning from each other, and talking about the future in Eastern and Western Europe. During meals, Romanian Baptist women sat next to Greek Orthodox women, while German Pentecostal women passed the butter to Polish Evangelical women. I had never seen such camaraderie between strangers.

Every day we had a short devotion, a teaching session, a prayer time, and a report. Women explained their homelands' situations: talking about the needs, the ministry opportunities, and prayer requests. Women, once divided, were now inspiring each other to change our European continent for Christ. They spoke passionately about reaching its 620 million people with the good news of Jesus' freedom and forgiveness. I sat in humble worship—this was indeed a beautiful portrait of the power of a united body of Christ.

At the beginning of the week, women from the East were quite shy. They spoke of the hardships suffered as Christians: how their children were ridiculed in school and quite often lost privileges. How this often caused the moms to struggle with guilt: "Because of our family's choice to follow Jesus, even our children are suffering." Inevitably each woman would close her report by saying, "But Jesus is worth it!"

We Westerners were humbled and inspired by the sacrifices these women were willing to make for their faith.

On the other hand, women from the East were surprised by all the creative ideas women from the West were using to reach the lost in their countries, including women's breakfast meetings, retreats, and publications. As I showed them covers of the Hungarian and Romanian *Lydia* magazines that would soon be printed and distributed, their eyes widened. Listening to their excited chatter, I chuckled to myself. Only a year ago, that had been the one minus on my list.

Yes, the magazines would help women in the East reach their nations with the gospel. Sparks of hope began to flicker in their eyes, and more dreams were born. I could read in their faces the hope, the idea of women's magazines for their nations.

During the evenings, different speakers challenged us with God's Word. The first evening it was my turn. I was excited to have this opportunity to mobilize women for world evangelism. I wanted women to find their gifts and use them—whether at home, at church, in their neighborhood, or in society. For too long, women had been silenced and discouraged. Yet, 70 percent of the church consists of women. I wanted to mobilize all the people in the church to help in the harvest—men, women, and children. I also had a keen desire to see female leaders who would model godliness in word, conduct, love, spirit, faith, and purity, based on the apostle Paul's words: "Don't let anyone look down on you because you are young, but set an example for the believers in speech, in conduct, in love, in faith and in purity."[45]

I asked God what I should talk about at this first-ever joining of East and West women. I prayed for a long time, and God put on my heart to speak about a woman's calling. For my illustrations, I used the example of European women of faith whom Jesus used greatly, such as Susanna Wesley, Catherine Booth, Corrie ten Boom, and Mother Teresa. "We can learn from these women who've gone before us," I said.

"What needs in your own countries could you attend to?" I asked the women. "Susanna, Catherine, Corrie, and Teresa were great Christian leaders who did not give in to fear. They used their gifts serving others; they leaned into God every time obstacles stood in their way. Clearly, their lives show that God delights in using all His children, including women, to play a vital role in His plan."

"What dreams has God given you?" I challenged the women. "Has He given you a pen to write, a hand to help, a mouth to speak, or an instrument to play? Use it and encourage others to get involved!"

We all knew we had been part of something historic that week. Forty women came together as strangers, and by the time we left, we were friends. Love, hope, and excitement had blossomed among us. As I watched women pray, hug, and exchange addresses at the end of the conference, I knew we would continue to meet! We realized we needed each other.

In April 1994, "Hope for Europe—Women in Leadership" met again, this time in Poland. Our theme was, "What Happens When Women Pray." After the Austrian meeting, word got out, and many more women wanted to attend. Deciding to keep it small, we sent invitations to around 180 women and were thrilled that nearly all of them were coming. But we began to wonder if there was a way to include more women.

The more laborers God raises up, I thought, *the more significant the impact across Europe.*

After praying about it, God put it on our hearts to have an open invitation for the last day of the conference. We rented a theater with about seven hundred seats. I was glad that my Polish friend, Alina Wieja, joined me in leadership and sent out invitations to Polish women.

Once again, the conference was a hit. On the last day, excited women from all walks of life filled the theatre—young, old, and everything in between. Polish young people led us with lively music. After the challenging messages, hundreds of women committed themselves to pray for the lost in Europe. We realized that, apart from prayer, our work is in vain.

In March 1997, we met in Budapest, the "Pearl of Eastern Europe." More than 180 women from 28 different countries attended the first part of the conference, which was only by invitation. We were amazed to hear what God was doing across the continent.

Ana from Romania moved many to tears as she told of her family's suffering. Yet Ana's attitude was terrific: Pain and suffering had not destroyed her faith in God; instead, it had become stronger. She continued to minister to other women in need.

A woman from Northern Ireland said, "We light candles when things get too rough."

A woman from the Netherlands held up some tulips as she said, "These tulips in my hand will be dead by Sunday. Why? They are cut off from the ground. This is the problem in Europe: There is no Christian soil left in which young people can grow roots. Pray for us: We need to build strong Christian homes!"

The last day of the conference topped our expectations. A year earlier, a coworker with the Hungarian *Lydia* and I had searched for a venue big enough. Finally, we found a hall which could seat 1,200. At first, we hesitated to rent it: both the size and the price made us gasp. Still, we felt that God had led us, and we would take the chance. Three weeks before the conference started, we already had three thousand women registered. Obviously, we needed to find a bigger place. So we booked the local sports arena in the city. We paid a large deposit and hoped that the three thousand registrants would show up; it was a considerable risk.

The last day of the Hungary "97 'Hope for Europe'" conference came, and as I arrived at the sports arena, I was dumbfounded. Busload after busload of women streamed into the stadium, filling it. Most of the women were from different parts of Hungary, but there were also busloads of women from Serbia, Romania, and other neighboring countries. Jill Briscoe challenged us with her message, and as a result, women were ready to go home and reach out to their cities and countries. Once again, God used our time together to break down denominational and organizational walls.

PLATFORM SHOES

There was a price to pay for my decade of leadership.
But the joy of walking with God
and seeing Him do miracles has been priceless.

Because of the "Hope for Europe" conferences, Christian women initiated various projects and began working together in their countries, despite their previous differences.

That was also true of the women in Germany. While twelve of us were a core committee, another forty women came from different backgrounds, spanning the spectrum from charismatic to conservative evangelical Christians, who worked together. At a meeting in Kassel, Germany, the group decided that Germany would like to be the host country for the next "Hope for Europe" conference in 1999.

Again, the committee and I had to decide what size of the hall we should rent for the conference's last day. The women estimated that we would need a building with a maximum capacity of 1,200 seats. "We'll be lucky to fill it," they said.

I understood their hesitation to rent anything larger, for our finances were low. Still, my experience in Budapest had shown me that it's better to rent a larger building early than to try and find one three weeks before the conference begins. When I voiced this, a woman suggested a building in Frankfurt that could seat about five thousand people. "In case we don't get that many, the building can be divided," she said. We agreed to rent it and signed the contract.

Three months before the conference, we already had ten thousand women registered for the final celebration day! Twice as many as our venue could accommodate. *Should we tell some women to stay at home? No, we would try to find a larger place.* Thankfully, we found a hall on the Frankfurt exhibition and trade fairgrounds available for the weekend we needed. It was an absolute miracle, as the venue was usually booked two years in advance.

My hand was shaking as Ditmar and I signed the papers. Since "Hope for Europe" was not registered as an organization in Germany, we had to sign, showing that we were taking full responsibility for the cost, which was horrendous! We were not charging for the event; therefore, there were no ticket sales. We depended solely on a freewill offering from the women.

At that moment, I realized that feeling fear is different from following fear. I felt fear, all right, but I chose not to follow it. David, in Scripture, was an excellent example for me as he stood before Goliath. It was not how well he fought but how well he believed. Our leadership team was excited. But it was the kind of excitement that is accompanied by an overwhelming thought: *What have we gotten ourselves into?*

As I looked over the thousands of women gathered in Frankfurt's beautiful concert hall, the life and joy in that room were overwhelming. The auditorium and the balconies were full. I looked out over the diverse crowd: women of all backgrounds and ages, women in dresses, young girls in jeans, and Lutheran sisters were wearing their caps.

Although most of the participants came from German-speaking countries, godly female leaders representing thirty-two European countries launched the meeting with a march of flags. As they carried their flags down the aisles, the place felt like holy ground. The women positioned the flags around a huge wooden cross that stood on the platform. At this moment, some women took their shoes off, recognizing the presence of the Lord.

Then they knelt down and asked God to have mercy on our continent. As I watched them, I remembered my prayer years ago for *Lydia* and God's amazing response: "Ask of me, and I will give you the nations as an inheritance." Never did I expect Him to answer in such a way! None of us on the committee had dreamed of such an overwhelming response. Even with the best advertisement strategy, we could not have "produced" such a result.

Gigi Tchividjian Graham and Elke Werner, along with others, challenged the women to use their gifts, no matter the size. Shirinai Dosova, a former Muslim from Moscow, shared how she had become a Christian and urged everyone: "Let us share the gospel! Let us love people as Christ loves them. That alone is our purpose for living." As an opportunity for salvation was made, more than three hundred women responded. The conference hours passed all too quickly, but the memory of thousands of women gathered together in prayer and mutual trust in God has left a lasting impression.

When we took the offering, I was a bit nervous. We had asked some men to be our ushers and to count the money. Later, Ditmar stepped onto the platform to tell us the amount. With tears in his eyes, he said we had more than enough to cover the entire cost of the conference!

Something funny happened to the men as they drove to the bank to deposit the money. In a random inspection, the police stopped their vehicle. When the police found out that the men carried a large amount of cash in small bills, they became suspicious.

"I don't have anything to do with this!" one of the ushers exclaimed nervously. "All I did was count the money!"

It took a while to explain the situation, but finally, the police let the men go, and they were able to deposit the money in the bank.

After covering the conference costs, we had enough money left over to support women from Eastern Europe who wanted to attend a worldwide conference and the following meeting in Budapest in 2002. God blessed us abundantly, and He continues to bless us beyond our imagination.

When the Frankfurt hall lights were off and the doors closed behind us, we went back to our own countries and the daily tasks waiting for us. Recharged, these women carried the good news of Jesus. They determined to let their lights shine in their cities and countries. Today these women are changing the world; in Moscow, teaching the Bible at a seminary; in Budapest, leading a women's conference; in Bucharest, serving the poor; and in Belarus, bringing down the abortion rate.

Indeed, when God told me to ask for the nations, I never would have expected this. God took what little I invested by saying "yes" to Him and multiplied it beyond my imagination. Over the decade of my leadership in "Hope for Europe" conferences, there was a price to pay. But the joy of walking with God and seeing Him do miracles has been priceless.

I do admit that I did not always leave the battles to the Lord. My weakened body left me so emotionally and physically drained that I sometimes felt I had more than I could handle. Looking back now, I wish I had trusted God more. Has God ever lost a battle? No! God doesn't lose battles. He reminded me, "Anyone signing up for the kingdom of God has to go through plenty of hard times."[46] It goes with the job.

As Stephen R. Covey said in his book *Everyday Greatness*: "Whether working independently or teaming with others, we can expect opposition. How we choose to respond to adversity can make or break our ability to accomplish the purposes we choose to pursue. Fortunately, much of the opposition we face in life ultimately works in our favor. It challenges us. It teaches us. It causes us to reach a little higher and to dig a little deeper."[47]

I agree. I realize that when I face challenges, it is time to pray. One of my favorite prayers is: "God grant me the serenity to accept the things I cannot change, courage to change the things I can, and wisdom to know the difference."[48]

A year later, I knew it was time to pass my leadership position on to someone else. Besides, many of the women in other European countries were starting their own conferences to encourage women to reach out to their own nations, cities, and towns.

Hope for Europe—Women in Leadership celebrated their 25th anniversary in 2018 in Belgrade, Serbia. I had the privilege to be a keynote speaker. A video presentation made for the occasion depicting the history of Hope for Europe amazed me and made me thankful that I had said yes to Lorry—and even more to God.

One thing I know for sure: no matter what I do, for the rest of my life, I want to pursue knowing God more, so I will become a woman after His heart. And I want to encourage other women in this pursuit.

DANCING ON HOLY GROUND

At age fifty-three, I finally discovered the missing pieces of my life's puzzle. I wasn't who I thought I was.

Standing at my father's grave in 1983, I felt cheated as I watched the coffin lowered into the grave. They forever buried my chance for his approval and love under a pile of dirt. As I was trying to comfort my sister Edit, who was weeping bitterly, she pulled away from me. "You don't understand what it means to lose a father!" she said angrily.

What did that mean? I couldn't ask her then. It was not the time. But I always wondered afterward, *Should I ask her what she meant by that?*

I could no longer avoid the truth about my identity. Clues were everywhere, and I kept wondering what the story was behind them.

When a dear friend visited me in 1998, we spent days catching up on each other's news. Then our conversation turned to my childhood, and she asked me how I felt about my mother and father. Finally, she said, "Elizabeth, last night, I prayed long and thought a lot." She hesitated, then spoke softly. "As a counselor, I feel I need to tell you that I believe the man who raised you was not your father."

"Not my father?" I echoed her. Then I remembered Edit's comment at Dad's funeral.

Maybe that was the essence of the fear I buried with my father, I thought. Then other questions bombarded my mind: *If he wasn't my father, then who was my father? Why would my mother never tell me? Who am I?*

I pushed these thoughts into the deepest recesses of my mind. But they wouldn't stay there. The raw pain of my questions—my lack of identity—kept creeping into my life like an uninvited visitor. *My mother is still alive,* I thought. *I could ask her.* But then, at her age, I worried the stress of the conversation would be too much for her fragile health.

I wonder if I could get advice from Lydia? I thought.

In the magazine, we carry an advice column where people can ask questions about life and relationships. *Our readers feel free to ask questions,* I thought. *So now it's my turn.*

I made my question anonymous and sent it to the columnist: "Everything seems to point to the fact that my father was not my biological father. I keep wondering, *Who am I? Where do I belong? Why am I different?* If I knew the answer to these questions, I think I would experience relief from an overwhelming pain that I have never known my true father."

When the columnist's answer arrived at the office, I grabbed the paper, ran home, and read her advice: "Secrets have a great bearing on a family. That is what you felt in your family. These indirect messages must have been very confusing for a little girl. Now the secret has come to light. This is a good thing because now you can move toward healing."

I couldn't believe how aptly the columnist was describing the perplexity and depth of my confusion. *Yes, I hoped healing would come soon, but how?* I continued reading: "Your grief is reasonable and can be compared to death. Allow yourself a time of mourning. Pour out your grief before Jesus. He understands you. He is crying with you. He will walk with you through the dark night of pain."

Then she reminded me of my Heavenly Father, our Creator, Who watches over us all our lives. "He is your true Father," she said. As I let this truth wash over me like a warm shower, it brought me some peace.

I kept telling myself that God had chosen this particular earthly family for me. Moreover, He had carefully chosen two individuals to be my parents, who would give me the genetic makeup I needed. I was not an accident; I was His custom-made creation. I knew this from

God's Word: "The days of my life [were] all prepared before I'd even lived one day."[49] Even my nationality was not an accident.

Both the columnist's answer and God's Word gave me the courage to call Edit, my older sister. "Edit, maybe one day, I want to write about my life," I began. "So I would like to know more about my childhood. Since you are nine years older than I am, you know much more than I do, may I ask you some questions?"

She agreed. But as I kept asking about our family, I sensed Edit was holding something back from me.

"Edit," I interrupted her nice little story, "something is missing! You're not telling me the whole story."

Silence. All I heard was a low hissing on the telephone line.

"I don't think I should tell you this," Edit said hesitantly with a pinched voice.

"Please, God," I prayed under my breath. "Don't let her tell me anything that is not true. I want to know the truth!"

"Please, Edit," I said. "Tell me all of it!"

After a deep sigh, she said bluntly, "Our father is not your father."

"How do you know that?" I asked. Now that I had my presumptions confirmed, I wanted to know the details. I hoped it would help explain the mysteries of my upbringing.

"I sometimes overheard Mother talking with her oldest sister," Edit continued. "They thought I was sleeping, but I was wide awake and heard every word they were saying. When I was eighteen, Mother gave me a photo of a man. 'Keep this for me, please,' she said. 'Someday, somebody will look for this photo.'"

"Is that all you know about my father?" I asked.

"Well, I know a little bit more, but not too much," Edit continued. "Apparently, Mother loved a certain young man, but her mother, our grandmother, wanted her to marry Father, who was a rich widower. So, under Grandma's pressure, Mom married Dad. A year later, I was born, and then Rosie. One day, Mom and Dad fought and, in a fit of rage, he sent Mother away."

It was unbelievable. My suspicions were confirmed, but I had no idea about all these baffling details. "Mother walked for days to get to her parents' house," Edit continued. "And in their town, she met your birth father again. His wife had just died. They began to visit each other frequently and were talking of marriage."

Edit stopped her narration to give me a chance to comment. "Why did she return to Dad instead of staying with the man she loved?"

"Well, your father was drafted to go to war," Edit explained. "While he was away, he was injured and hospitalized. He wrote Mom several letters, but she never received them. Uncle Pista hid the letters because he wanted Mom to return to Dad, who was now begging her to come back home. At first, Mom didn't know what to do. But since she hadn't heard anything from your father, she returned to Dad."

"And was she pregnant with me at that time?"

"Yes," my sister said. "Everybody advised her to abort you. They said it was because she was sick with diphtheria, but I think they wanted her to abort because you weren't Dad's child."

It was one thing to be curious about my true identity. It was quite another to hear the details. The truth sounded stranger than fiction. But right then, I wished it were fiction. Hearing these details made me feel like everything I had ever known or felt about myself was fake. I desperately wanted to file all this new information in my brain to process it at some convenient date, but there was no file folder for it. Furthermore, I felt as if a tornado had swept through my brain, scattering all of my neatly organized files into disarray.

I asked what seemed only natural to ask next: "Is my father still alive?"

"No," Edit replied.

"No?" I repeated her answer, hoping she would tell me more. But she didn't.

The tears I had managed to hold off now cascaded down my cheeks. *That couldn't be my story. Maybe this was just a misunderstanding or a nightmare.*

Later that night, I tearfully recounted the whole story to Ditmar. "I don't even know who I am," I cried. "I am not the person I thought I was all these years." Ditmar took me into his strong arms and comforted me.

I was tired and worn out and confused. Yet life continued. The imminent demands of the magazine and leadership responsibilities were screaming for my attention. Though I wanted the world to stop, it did not. And, typical of shocking grief, there were times when all was well, and I felt normal; then, amid a mundane task, raw emotion would overcome me, and I would sit and sob.

"Heavenly Father," I prayed, "hold me and strengthen me. How thankful I am to have You as my Father. Thank You for adopting me into Your family. You said in the Bible, 'I will be a Father to you, and you will be my sons and daughters.'[50] You have taken care of me. You are the best Father—no earthly father could ever compete with You."

The day after my phone call with Edit, Ditmar said, "I have a surprise for you." He handed me a box. "Unpack it."

I unwrapped the paper and held a plaque in my hand. It said, *This certifies that Elizabeth Mittelstaedt is a subject of biographical record in Who's Who in the World, 1998.*

I stared at the plaque practically in a stupor. "How on earth did I get this?" I said aloud. "Who knows who I am? I don't even know myself!"

Then the Holy Spirit whispered gently to my heart: "I know you! In this whole wide world, I see you, and I just wanted to let you know." How comforting it was for me when I read in the Bible in the book of Jeremiah, "Before I shaped you in the womb, I knew all about you. Before you saw the light of day, I had holy plans for you."[51]

Through the years, I have received many awards, but the timing of this one was remarkable.

The plaque alone did not stop my ongoing struggle with my identity. I continued to ask God to give me the freedom to understand the "me" He had created.

God did not throw out my past; neither did He tell me to forget about it. Instead, He used the material and rearranged it so that it became new. He didn't waste my pain either but turned it into compassion for others, so I could help them become free of guilt and regret.

Although healing took time, I was grateful I could place everything into the Healer's hands. And I was thankful that, despite the new revelation about my birth father, I had a good relationship with my mother. She was growing in faith just as much as I was, which was wonderful.

One morning, as I listened to the beautiful words of the song "This Is My Father's World," my heart became so overwhelmed with His love that I jumped to my feet and took my shoes off. As if I were standing on holy ground.

I had searched so long for the love of a father. And I had found it at last, and I understood it.

I know who I am! I am adopted by the Most High God. Jesus Christ became poor that I might become rich—that I might be adopted into His royal family and become a co-heir of the kingdom of God with Him. So I am a child of the king of kings. That means I am a princess. My dream as a little girl has become a reality, after all!

OPEN-TOED SECRETS

Life is shaped by God's promises—and His startling surprises. But it is up to us what we do with both.

A year passed after the revealing conversation with my sister. My mother, now eighty-three, invited me to spend some time with her in Budapest. One morning, as we were sitting on a sofa, drinking coffee, she said, "I want to tell you that I love you very much, my dear daughter. Thank you for taking care of me financially in my old age, and thank you for helping your younger sisters so they could complete their education."

After a short pause, she continued, "It may be that I won't live much longer, and before I die, I want to tell you something." She looked at me earnestly. "I have told you earlier that I gave birth to you in great pain and that people advised me to abort you because of sickness. I am so thankful that God kept me from doing that."

Tears filled her eyes. "There is something else you need to know because it is part of your life," my mother continued. "It wouldn't be right to take this secret with me to the grave."

The following seconds of silence seemed like an eternity. I let her talk and, even though I knew some of the details already, I listened patiently.

"The father who raised you was not your biological father," my mother said.

Hearing my mother say those words pierced my heart afresh. I guess I had hoped, somehow, that the story of my identity wasn't real after all. Now my mother confirmed it.

"When your father came back from the war, he visited me and asked me why I did not wait for him," my mother said. "I told him I had not received any news from him. Later, we found out that your uncle Pista had hidden the letters from me. Your father begged me to return to him. His wife had died, and he wanted us to be together, along with his two sons."

"Why didn't you go back to my birth father?"

"One day, I went to a Catholic church and, while taking communion, thought about what would happen if I divorced my husband and married your father. As a Catholic, I would never again be able to take communion."

"Did my real father ever see me?" I asked.

"Yes," Mom replied. "When you were about six months old, I took you with me on a visit to my older sister. When I boarded the train to return home, I did not realize your father was on the same train. He saw me holding a baby and knew it was his baby daughter. Suddenly our eyes met. He came over and took you into his arms and hugged you close to his chest. With a gentle look in his eyes, he handed you back to me and said, 'Please watch over little Elizabeth. Take good care of her.' You were his only daughter, you know. He had two sons: one of them was Beni."

Beni! My childhood playmate whom I adored. When I had announced to my aunt that one day I would marry Beni, she had said most forcefully, "You can marry anyone in the whole wide world—but not Beni!" Now I understood why. But even back then, I had loved him—because he was my brother!

"Your father saw you whenever you visited my sister," Mom continued. "Do you remember fetching water from the fountain?"

"Yes."

"Well, you always walked by your father's house, and he would stand at the window watching you."

Yes, I remembered. *I had sometimes wondered why he was staring at me like that.*

Mother and I sat in silence, letting decades of secrecy and mystery sink in. All I could think to say to her were the same words she had told me so many times: "I'm not here by accident. Every scene of my life was written in God's book before it happened. He has a plan for my life! That is why He brought me to this earth, and He placed me into the Radnics family. I believe He picked this place for me for a purpose."

But now I understood the rejection I fought all my life and my craving to be loved: I was rejected in the womb. The deepest wound of the human spirit is to be rejected. Even Jesus experienced rejection: "He was despised and rejected by mankind, a man of suffering, and familiar with pain."[52] How glad I was that Jesus bore my rejection so I could have His acceptance. What a privilege it is to know God and have peace with Him!

I looked at my mother with a new appreciation. Despite the dangers, fears of reproach, and grievous loss, she chose to give me life.

"Thank you for telling me," I leaned toward her and looked deeply into her eyes. "I love you even more now."

"Tell the story, Elizabeth," she said simply. "Maybe it will help someone else avoid some pitfalls in life."

I wished my mother good night and walked to my room.

I thought again about my mother's words: "Tell your story, Elizabeth. Maybe others will learn how to avoid some pitfalls in life."

It took time for me to write my story in order to bring healing and liberation to those who are suffering. A primary key in my recovery was finding my voice—the voice I never had as a little girl. I wrote to encourage others. There was hope, and life was worth living beyond past pains.

Yes, life has knocked me down multiple times. But with God's strength, I did not stay down. I bounced back. Each day I draw strength from God's Word, which gives me the encouragement and challenge I need to overcome life's difficulties.

While suffering has been part of my past, and the why of it may not make sense until I get to heaven, it is in God's hands, not mine, and definitely not in the hands of those who wronged me. When I let go of the painful memories, at last, I understand what true freedom is: submitting my will to His and accepting His leading in complete dependency on Him. Total surrender to my heavenly Father has brought me a peace that passed all understanding. For, you see, peace is not the absence of trouble; it is God's presence in the midst of trouble. There are many ways to be enslaved, but there is only one way to be set free: by the power of grace and the Holy Spirit, who truly healed my soul. After all, He gave me back my health and healed my wounds, just like He promised. Why some pain remained, I didn't know. I didn't understand, at least not yet.

My true identity, then, is defined by God, not by others. I admit many things in my life have been taken from me. However, one thing will remain, the freedom to choose how I react.

So how should I then think of my past? Not remembering it would mean losing a huge chunk of me. Would I be the same person without these painful experiences? Did these experiences not shape me and make me who I am? Had I not suffered, would I now have compassion for women who are suffering? God has used my suffering for His higher purpose: to birth magazines that reach women in many nations.

Just like the Psalmist says: "So those who planted their crops in despair will shout hurrahs at the harvest, so those who went off with heavy hearts will come home laughing, with armloads of blessing."[53] Each day I'm amazed at the depth of joy God provides, even in the midst of pain.

In *Walking in My Shoes*, I followed my journey from country to country, continent to continent, and from one experience to another.

Besides the unexpected bends in the road and the cliff-hanging moments, I have glimpsed, without a shadow of a doubt, God's guidance and goodness to me. Whenever I needed help, He was there, taking charge.

My journey is not finished yet. As I keep traveling with my heavenly Father as my guide, I keep wondering: *What's up ahead? What will the scenery be? Will it be like the lush German countryside, with its green pastures where cows graze, or breathtaking mountains and valleys where flowers grow? Or will I at times wander through the dryness of the desert— and see brief glimpses of rare beauty in the cactus flowers?*

Yes, throughout the years, eternity has become a topic of great interest to me. What seems so unfair in this life will be made right in eternity. So sufferings are not everlasting. What is everlasting is God's love and mercy.

"Is Beni still alive?" I asked my sister Edit.

"No, he died a few years ago."

She walked into the living room to get her purse, then pulled out a small photograph and handed it to me. It was a photo of my father— all I would ever see of him. But I will also forever hold in my heart the image my mother shared with me—of my father holding me gently in his arms when he saw me with my mother on the train.

I've come to realize that I have had three fathers: My heavenly Father, who knit me together in my mother's womb; my birth father, who gave me life; and my other earthly father, who reared me and gave me a home. As I thought about this, thankfulness and love for him filled my heart.

When I get to heaven, after I've hugged you, Jesus, I will run to my earthly father and thank him for allowing me to stay in his house for the first eighteen years of my life. Maybe he, now redeemed, will tell me those words I have been longing to hear: "Elizabeth, I do love you."

But I want to be very clear: Although I've taken a long look into my past and written about it in this book, I no longer dwell there. I have left my regrets behind, choosing to remember only the ones that were redeemed. Out of my experiences have come lessons of growth— and sneak peeks at God's goodness and His amazing grace.

I look back at all the shoes I've walked in during my life's journey, and I realize how far I've come. I've known great depths of heartache. But I've known even greater heights of God's love and sustaining power.

God has truly put a spring in my step. I have a lot to celebrate. It's time now to put on my running shoes because I've not only survived, I've overcome.

EPILOGUE

True Freedom

When I was growing up, at harvest time, everyone in my village had to bring in the crops. With concentrated effort, we labored diligently to reap the fruit of the fields before it became ruined by rain or before a thunderstorm lashed the wheat to the ground, where it became nearly impossible to harvest.

Everyone was needed—not just a few strong men. My father was responsible for cutting the wheat with a sickle, and my mother gathered the stalks into a bundle. My task as a little girl was to carry the cords with which my father tied up the bundles. During the harvest time, I saw our village people reunite in a new and powerful alliance every year. Without harvest time, we would have continued to meander in our little dramas, unaware of the joys and needs that existed beyond us.

Likewise, in the global harvest of souls, everyone is needed, and every contribution is critical. God gave us a select circle of friends who carried this crucial work with their prayers and support. Through the years, my sisters and my husband have cheered me on. Their prayers have kept me warm when cold winds of trouble have blown into my face and when financial or health problems have knocked me down. Because of these faithful prayer warriors, God has blessed us and enlarged our territory. Each person has had a significant impact on the harvest, and I know God will reward them greatly.

I don't know what part you will play in the harvest of the twenty-first century. The important thing is to lean into God and ask Him.

The greatest thing I have done in my life is to repeatedly entrust my many questions to God—even though I haven't received answers to all of them. The Creator enriched my tumultuous journey.

I have seen God do immeasurably more than I could ask, imagine, or dream, through the printed page and through choosing the countries where Ditmar and I should live and work. How wonderful now to see the fruition of the dream God gave me to share His good news with the nations. Not all my dreams have been fulfilled. But I offer them to the One who is bigger than my dreams.

As I write these pages, thankfulness overwhelms me. I am doing so much better healthwise now than in the years before. God has also restored my wounded soul. "In the valley he restores my soul," David wrote in Psalm 23. It does not mean that I am living without pain. But I will not lose hope even if I have to wait. I know, with God, I'm in a "win-win" situation: the victory will come either here on earth or there in heaven.

In Hebrews, chapter 11 is often referred to as the "gallery of faith." It mentions two groups. Group One escaped the sword, and Group Two died from it. We'd all like to be in Group One, wouldn't we? But the Bible says that both groups gained God's approval through their faith.

How did they do it? They saw the end goal way off in the distance. Their faith kept them focused.

My faith, too, has kept me focused. I have decided to live one day at a time. I know God has not wasted my pain or my dreams. More often than not, I've discovered the two intertwine. I also know that my relationship with my heavenly Father is not based on performance but love. I want to please Him by loving Him.

I wish I could have left out of these pages my failures and the vulnerable parts, but then pieces of me would have been missing. Perhaps some readers will learn from my mistakes and avoid some failures of their own. Maybe a reader will be drawn closer to the Savior and experience the freedom and forgiveness He gives. Then it was all worth it. I've tried to record my story as accurately as I remember it and to tell the essence of it in these short pages. I understand that being honest carries some risk, but I choose to help others find their freedom from the past.

Through the years, my weakness has become a showcase of His power. "But we have this treasure in jars of clay (a cracked pot—yes, that's me!) to show that this all-surpassing power is from God and not from us."[54]

It was God's grace that took my pain and brought some good out of it. What an amazing God He is! As the psalmist, David says, "God rewrote the text of my life when I opened the book of my heart to his eyes."[55]

My desire is no longer: What can God give me? But: What can I offer Him? I want to express my deep love and thankfulness for His continued faithfulness and strength. I want to stay on His path and finish well so that one day it can be said of me: "She served God's purpose in her generation."

As I've taken this journey to reflect on my life, I've been amazed to find how often it was during the times of most profound failures and disappointment—when I thought it was all over—God led me into greater intimacy and calling. So, do not despise the dark places of death to self and death to dreams. They are a pathway to His abundant life, a life of faith, freedom, and forgiveness. God never wastes our pain. In the mysterious methodology of the Messiah, He always takes it and turns it into a redemptive blessing—usually for the saving of others and to increase worship of and reliance upon God, which, of course, is the point of the harvest.

God is a relentless pursuer of hurting souls. I know that because He has pursued me. I know that, also, because of the thousands of letters I have read. Women have written how Jesus spoke gently and graciously to them while wandering through their own deserts of pain. He is the only One who can turn our valleys of trouble into a door of hope and true freedom. He is bigger than our dreams.

—Elizabeth

ENDNOTES

1 Roman 3:10 NIV
2 Ephesians 2:8-9 NIV
3 Luke 15:21-23 NIV
4 Matthew 6:12 NLT
5 Psalm 9:9-10 MSG
6 Proverbs 4:23 NIV
7 Isaiah 64:8 NIV
8 Isaiah 52:7 NIV
9 Song of Solomon 2:10-12 NIV
10 Ruth 1:16-17 NIV
11 *Free of Charge: Giving and Forgiving in a Culture Stripped of Grace* by Miroslav Volf, Zondervan, 2005
12 Proverbs 19:2 NLT
13 *The Life You Always Wanted* by John Ortberg, Zondervan Publishing, 2002
14 1 Peter 1:18-19 NIV
15 James 5:14-15 NIV
16 Jeremiah 30:17 NIV
17 Psalm 10:1 NIV
18 1 Corinthians 10:13 NIV
19 Isaiah 49:15 NIV
20 See Psalm 23:4 NKJV
21 Job 13:15 NIV
22 Isaiah 53:5 NIV
23 Job 2:6 NIV
24 *Quest Study Bible*, Zondervan, 1994
25 Psalm 118:24 NKJV

[26] Isaiah 30:15 NIV

[27] Matthew 6:34 NIV

[28] Psalm 56:8 NLT

[29] Hebrews 11:1 NIV

[30] Psalm 2:8 NIV

[31] Ruth 2:10 MSG

[32] Isaiah 54:1 NIV

[33] *Morning Devotional* by D.L. Moody, Whitaker House, 2001

[34] Luke 15:9-10 MSG

[35] John 3:16 NKJV

[36] Ephesians 6:11-17 NIV

[37] *Integrity* by Dr. Henry Cloud, Harper Collins Publishers, 2006

[38] Psalm 2:8 NIV

[39] Psalm 50:10 NIV

[40] *When Someone You Love Is Dying*, by Ruth Kopp, M.D., Zondervan, 1980

[41] Jeremiah 23:29 NIV

[42] Acts 2:28 MSG

[43] Genesis 2:18 NIV

[44] Matthew 25:36 NIV

[45] 1 Timothy 4:12 NIV

[46] Acts 14:22 MSG

[47] *Everyday Greatness* by Stephen R. Covey, Rutledge Hill Press, 2006

[48] *Book of Prayers and Services for the Armed Forces* by Reinhold Niebuhr, 1944

[49] Psalm 139:16 MSG

[50] 2 Corinthians 6:18 NIV

[51] Jeremiah 1:5 MSG

[52] Isaiah 53:3 NIV

[53] Psalm 126:5-6 MSG

[54] 2 Corinthians 4:7 NIV

[55] Psalm 18:24 MSG

ABOUT THE AUTHOR

Elizabeth Mittelstaedt has a unique and intriguing view on the world since she was born in Eastern Europe, and lived in Canada, the United States, the last forty years in Germany and recently she moved back to California.

Elizabeth is the Founder and Editor of *Lydia*, a Christian magazine for women, currently published in three languages: German, Hungarian, and Romanian. Since its initial launch in the German language in 1986, over 11 million copies have been distributed to eager readers in over 100 countries. Elizabeth speaks Hungarian, German, and English.

She is also the founder of the unparalleled "Hope for Europe— Women in Leadership" conferences, which linked arms with the Lausanne Committee for World Evangelization and the World Evangelical Fellowship Commission on Women's Concerns. For over a decade, Elizabeth led these groundbreaking training events, galvanizing and uniting women in both Eastern and Western Europe so they would take leadership in their own countries.

Over the years, Elizabeth has been instrumental in compiling numerous books, including women's devotional Bibles. She and her life story were featured on the cover of *Today's Christian Woman* in the US, and in *Eva*, in the Netherlands, amongst others.

Elizabeth was included in the *Who's Who in the World*. She was recognized by the International Biographical Centre in Cambridge as one of the "Outstanding People of the 20th Century" for her contribution to Christian women and other recognitions.

Rarely does someone come along who has the ability to bridge the gap between so many women of different cultures. But Elizabeth does this by connecting her own life journey and challenges to the quintessential questions and hearts of women, no matter their nationality and culture. Elizabeth's passion and lifetime focus is to help others overcome difficulties, as well as to inspire individuals to live a full life—a life greater than they've ever dreamed. A life packed with passion and purpose.

CPSIA information can be obtained
at www.ICGtesting.com
Printed in the USA
FSHW020518240621
82635FS